GW00671045

• HALSGROVE DISCOVER SERIES ➤

Jane Austen's HAMPSHIRE

TERRY TOWNSEND

HALSGROVE

First published in Great Britain in 2014

Copyright © Terry Townsend 2014

All rights reserved. No part of this publication may be
reproduced, stored in a retrieval system, or transmitted
in any form or by any means without the prior permission
of the copyright holder

British Library Cataloguing-in-Publication Data
A CIP record for this title is available from the British Library

ISBN 978 0 85704 233 0

HALSGROVE
Halsgrove House, Ryelands Business Park,
Bagley Road, Wellington, Somerset TA21 9PZ
Tel: 01823 653777   Fax: 01823 216796
email: sales@halsgrove.com

Part of the Halsgrove group of companies.
Information on all Halsgrove titles is
available at: www.halsgrove.com

Printed in China by
Everbest Printing Co Ltd

To Carol
who introduced me to Jane Austen
and walked with me in her steps

Jane Austen's Hampshire

*From the cradle of her talent
To the blossoming of her genius*

Terry Townsend

Acknowledgements

I would particularly like to thank;
Adrienne Bradney-Smith for generously sharing her knowledge
and advising on the manuscript as a whole.
Brenda Stables for her encouragement and editorial help.

I would also like to admit the debt I owe
to the scholarship of Deirdre Le Faye plus the help I received from
David Rymill of the Hampshire Archives and Local Studies
and Andrew Jose of the Basingstoke Discovery Centre.

The following local Hampshire historians made a valuable contribution:
Jane Hurst from Alton Museum and
Richard Waldram and Peter Baker from Overton.
Thank you too for the courtesy and cooperation extended by Jane Austen's House Museum,
Chawton, Alton, Hampshire GU34 1SD www.jane-austens-house-museum.org.uk
and Chawton House Library, Chawton, Alton, Hampshire GU34 1SJ www.chawton.org

Contents

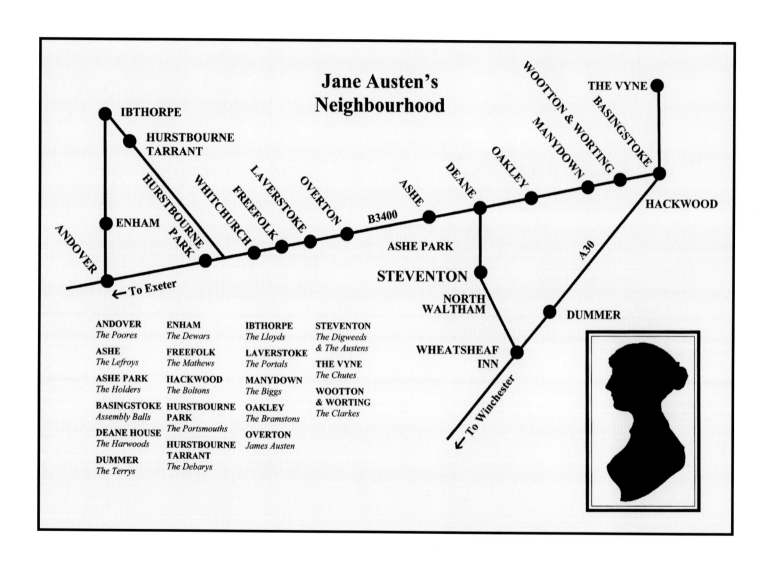

Jane Austen's Neighbourhood

IBTHORPE

HURSTBOURNE TARRANT

THE VYNE

WOOTTON & WORTING

BASINGSTOKE

MANYDOWN

OAKLEY

ASHE

DEANE

OVERTON

LAVERSTOKE

FREEFOLK

WHITCHURCH

HURSTBOURNE PARK

ENHAM

ANDOVER

HACKWOOD

B3400

ASHE PARK

STEVENTON

A30

← To Exeter

NORTH WALTHAM

DUMMER

WHEATSHEAF INN

← To Winchester

ANDOVER
The Poores

ASHE
The Lefroys

ASHE PARK
The Holders

BASINGSTOKE
Assembly Balls

DEANE HOUSE
The Harwoods

DUMMER
The Terrys

ENHAM
The Dewars

FREEFOLK
The Mathews

HACKWOOD
The Boltons

HURSTBOURNE PARK
The Portsmouths

HURSTBOURNE TARRANT
The Debarys

IBTHORPE
The Lloyds

LAVERSTOKE
The Portals

MANYDOWN
The Biggs

OAKLEY
The Bramstons

OVERTON
James Austen

STEVENTON
The Digweeds & The Austens

THE VYNE
The Chutes

WOOTTON & WORTING
The Clarkes

Introduction

IT IS A TRUTH universally acknowledged that a reader in possession of a good book gains further pleasure from knowing where the author lived, loved and found inspiration. In the case of Jane Austen, this was predominantly in Hampshire, the historic and beautiful county where she spent most of her days.

Jane Austen was born in 1775 in her father's rectory in the small village of Steventon. She grew to love the area and declared herself proud to be 'a Hampshire Austen'. During her early adulthood, spent mostly in the north of the county, Jane enjoyed a very full social life. Most of her friendships were formed during this time.

It was in her father's rectory that Jane wrote the first drafts of novels that were to become *Pride & Prejudice*, *Sense & Sensibility* and *Northanger Abbey*. The brilliant characters she created through observation of her family, friends and neighbours have remained relevant through the generations.

Jane's creative flow was interrupted in 1801 when, against her inclination, she was required to move to Bath, with her mother, father and sister Cassandra. The family stayed for only four of Jane's forty-one years. It was during this time she visited Lyme Regis and Devon on family holidays. Following Mr Austen's death in Bath in 1805 the three women returned home to Hampshire.

They settled temporarily into what was to be Jane's second Hampshire home. This was with Frank, one of her brothers, who was by then a naval captain renting spacious lodgings in Southampton. From here Jane made visits to the New Forest and Portsmouth.

Edward, another of her brothers, inherited the estate at Chawton near Alton, from the Knight family who were distant cousins of the Austens. It was at Chawton, in 1809, that Jane eventually settled with her mother and sister. They moved into the former bailiff's house where Jane was able to lead a quieter life and resume her novel writing which had been largely unproductive in the eight years since leaving Steventon.

Jane Austen's brilliant characters, created through observation of her Hampshire family, friends and neighbours, have remained relevant through the generations.

Samuel Grimm's watercolour of the Hampshire countryside is an evocative reminder of the landscape so dear to Jane.

The security of her third and last Hampshire home gave Jane the confidence to develop fully as a novelist. In the cottage at Chawton she wrote *Mansfield Park*, *Emma* and *Persuasion*, as well as revising *Sense & Sensibility* and *Pride & Prejudice*, published in 1811 and 1813 respectively. Publication of *Mansfield Park* and *Emma* followed in 1814 and 1816.

Early in 1817 she began work on *Sanditon*, but became ill and moved in the spring to Winchester, to be closer to the doctor who was treating her. Jane died on 18 July and was buried in Hampshire, in the nave of the grand cathedral at Winchester. *Northanger Abbey* and *Persuasion* were published posthumously. All of her novels had been conceived and written in Hampshire.

Many authors like Thomas Hardy and the Brontë sisters immortalised the predominant landscape of their life's experience. With Jane Austen the opposite is the case. There is near silence from her on the subject of the county which played such a major role in her life. She mentions Hampshire in only one of her works, when Fanny Price, the heroine of *Mansfield Park*, visits her parents in Portsmouth.

This may seem strange but on reflection, it is in keeping with her character and her desire for anonymity during the time she remained unsure of any lasting success. Luckily for us she was a prolific letter writer and a number of the Hampshire letters between Jane and her sister Cassandra have survived. Additional rich sources of information come from letters between family members and friends and two memoirs, one by her nephew James Edward and another by her niece Anna.

Hampshire is a county of contrasting and beautiful countryside. In the north are the green sweeping downs. Running through its centre are the lazy river valleys of the Itchen and Test, which flow gently into the sea along the busy coast.

It is a county to explore and enjoy and I can think of no better way to do this than to follow in the steps of Jane Austen. You will discover market towns where she shopped and villages where she visited friends to take tea, country parks where she strolled and country houses where she danced.

With a little imagination we can picture her boating on river creeks along the Solent and walking through the ancient city streets of Winchester and Southampton. We can walk with her and Fanny Price along the ramparts of Portsmouth, the spiritual home of the Royal Navy.

Hampshire provided the cradle for Jane Austen's talent and the peace and stability for the blossoming of her genius.

Jane declared herself proud to be 'a Hampshire Austen'.

Deane

During his Oxford years George Austen was known as 'the handsome proctor'. This portrait shows that Jane's father retained his good looks into retirement.

SIX MILES WEST of Basingstoke, along the B3400, stands an old road-side hostelry. It had been standing here, by the junction with Steventon Lane, for at least a century before the toll road was created in 1754. From that time it became known as Deane Gate Inn.

On Friday 27 April 1764 the note of a post horn alerted the gatekeeper of the approach of a coach and four. Two of the passengers, who had been jostled and buffeted for the last dozen miles, were newlyweds, George and Cassandra Austen.

Married in Bath the day before, they set off straightway for Hampshire. Their honeymoon night had been spent at an inn in Andover. Now they finally arrived at the hamlet of Deane, a little jaded from the journey but eager to begin their new life.

As they watched the coach depart, the couple smiled at each other in the delight of stretching aching limbs. Cassandra was twenty-five. She was wearing a red travelling dress made of hardwearing woollen fabric cut trimly in the style of a riding habit. George at thirty-three wore the unmistakable black attire of a parson. He was prepared to assume his duties as the parish priest of Deane and Steventon.

During their forthcoming life in the parish eight children would be born to them. One, a girl called Jane, was to earn a place among the best-known and best-loved authors in the world.

At the time the Austens were married, patronage was essential for a young man who desired a commission in the armed services or had aspirations to enter the church. The employment package of a vicar was referred to as a 'living' and livings were in the gift of wealthy landowners or landowning establishments like the cathedrals, the universities or the Crown.

Livings were sometimes bought and sold by the rich and powerful so they could bestow them on beneficiaries of their choice who were often the sons of distant relations. Jane Austen's novels are full of such examples. Obtaining a living was not a matter of becoming ordained and then applying for a vacancy.

Stagecoaches to and from London used the road through Deane twice a day. They were considered inappropriate transport for young ladies travelling alone which once led Jane to complain: 'I want to go in a stage coach, but Frank will not let me.'

The lane north from Steventon joins the present day B3400 at the staggered cross roads by the seventeenth-century inn. Austen family members would walk along the unmade lane to catch stagecoaches bound for Basingstoke or Exeter. We know that Jane's brother Charles was once unlucky enough to find the coach full and had to walk back home.

Jane's father had two Kentish relations to thank for his Oxford University education and his Hampshire clerical appointments. In 1761 Thomas Knight of Godmersham presented him with the 'living' of Steventon. And his great uncle Francis of Sevenoaks in Kent also purchased for him the living at Deane.

Pluralism, which enabled an incumbent to have the care (and income) of more than one parish was common at the time, though frowned on later. Absenteeism was another dubious but wide spread practice. A clergyman could live away from his parish and appoint a curate (at minimum wage) to undertake the duties. George Austen himself was absent for the first few years of his appointments. His move to the area was prompted by his marriage.

George's ultimate plan was to live in the Rectory at Steventon but that was in a dilapidated condition. For the first four years of their marriage, the Austens lived in Deane Parsonage whilst necessary repairs and alterations were undertaken to their intended home.

The Old Manor House at Deane, home to the Harwoods in Jane Austen's time.

Their first three children, James, George and Edward were all born at Deane. By 1768 Steventon Rectory had been extended and refurbished ready for the Austens to take up residence. Here, over the following eleven years, five more children were born; Henry, Cassandra, Francis, Jane and Charles.

In the spring of 1789 Revd George Austen let Deane Parsonage to Mrs Lloyd, the widow of a fellow clergyman. She moved in with her two oldest single daughters Mary and Martha. Over time these ladies became close friends of both Jane and her sister Cassandra. Jane was ten years younger than Martha but she came to consider her as a second sister.

On 27 March 1792, three years after the Lloyds moved to Deane, Jane's brother James, married Anne Mathew and he assumed the parish. It was therefore necessary for the Lloyds to move again. This time they moved to the village of Ibthorpe, 14 miles to the north west.

A daughter, Anna was born to James and Anne in 1793 but two years later Anne died quite unexpectedly. In 1797, James took Mary Lloyd as his second wife and so she moved back to Deane Parsonage, the house she had vacated five years earlier. James and Mary went on to have two children. Their son, James Edward, was born at Deane in 1798 and would, later in life, become Jane's first family biographer.

In 1801 Jane's parents made the decision to retire to Bath. James and his family then moved to Steventon Rectory where he became his father's curate. In 1805 Mary gave birth to a second child who was christened Caroline.

Nothing remains today of the old parsonage at Deane where Jane's parents began their married life. The church where her father and brother had both officiated is also gone. It was rebuilt after her death. The Old Manor House is still there, standing near the present church.

At the time of the Austens' association with Deane, the Manor House was home to John Harwood and his wife. The property had descended through a squirearchy of John Harwoods, fathers and sons, for five or six generations. The Harwoods were 'an old family with some racy peculiarities of character'. The novelist Henry Fielding used to visit nearby Oakley and it is generally supposed he modelled the character of the blustering Squire Western in *Tom Jones* on the John Harwood that the Austens knew.

Squire Western is a caricature of the rough-and-ready, conservative country gentleman who speaks in West Country dialect, and peppers his speech with curses. Fielding was a

Nothing remains of the old Deane Parsonage which was home for four years to the Reverend George Austen and his wife.
The church where Jane's father and brother officiated was rebuilt in Gothic style after her death.

novelist Jane admired although she could not quite forgive him for what she called his low standard on morals.

On 9 January 1796 Jane attended a ball at Deane Manor and in a letter to her sister Cassandra reported that she danced twice with John Willing Warren, once with Charles Watkins, and tells us that she: 'entirely escaped John Lyford. I was forced to fight hard for it, however. We had a very good supper, and the greenhouse was illuminated in a very elegant manner.'

John Harwood had a somewhat troublesome son called Earle in whose exploits Jane took an amused interest. Earle caused a stir by marrying a lady of doubtful reputation. He had apparently been told that his parents 'would receive his wife, if she continued to behave well for another year'. Jane reported that the couple lived 'in the most private manner at Portsmouth, without keeping a servant of any kind.'

Earle was an officer in the Royal Marines who held a supervisory position on one of the prison hulks moored in Portsmouth harbour. His problems were exacerbated when he managed to shoot himself in the leg. The direction of the wound meant it was unlikely to have been from the result of a duel. Luckily Haslar Hospital at Gosport was able to put him 'in a fair way of doing well' but the sorry business was a great consternation to the family at Deane.

By July 1818 the Norman church which Jane and her family had known was 'in so Dangerous state of Ruin as to be unsafe for the congregation.' Wither Bramston of Oakley Hall funded the building of the church you see today. It took a couple of years to construct at a cost of £8,000 and is made of Coade Stone, a cement-based material.

In contrast to the somewhat dull façade, the elegant interior has a handsomely ornamented chancel screen and stunning sanctuary window. It is described as the most complete and successful early nineteenth-century Gothic church in the county. Inside there are monuments to Hardwoods, Withers and Bramstons; all local families with whom Jane was on intimate terms.

Until recently Deane Manor had been owned by the Baring family of banking fame. Princess Margaret used to stay here despite the fact that she complained of being so disturbed by the church bells.

Steventon

NO BROWN TOURIST SIGN points the way to the corner of this quiet field, because there is nothing of significance to be seen. There is no memorial of any kind. No stone or plaque to mark the spot, just a slight depression of sodden ground where thistles grow in profusion and a small white notice warns in red letters DANGER KEEP OUT.

Steventon is slow, rural and unremarkable. At least it would be unremarkable but for one thing. This is the birthplace of one of England's best-known and best-loved novelists. Things around here have changed little in the two-hundred or so years since a friend of Jane's wrote her impression of the place:

15

'There is something pleasing and pastoral in the scenery hereabouts. Broken ground, green valleys, sheep-clad knolls, and gentle hills covered with wood, and openings through the boles of trees into the neighbouring open country, have a very delightful effect here, especially in the spring.'

Today dairy cattle graze on the open country where herds of sheep once wandered and most of the remaining land has been given over to arable crops. These things apart, the description remains true today. Such is the power and appeal of Jane Austen's novels that independent travellers from all over the world continue to make the pilgrimage to this place even though there is no visible trace of the house in which she was born.

By 1768 Steventon Rectory had been extended and refurbished ready for the Austens to take up residence. The condition of the side roads was pretty dire and James Austen recalls his mother having to recline on a feather mattress in the cart during the short journey when the family made the move from Deane.

In 1773, George decided to take boys 'of good family' as boarders, preparing them for university, where they would meet a largely classical syllabus. By 1774 three more of his

Below left: Recent research suggests this 1821 painting by Ben Lefroy is one of the cottages demolished in 1823 along with Steventon Rectory.

Below right: A plan of the Glebe land at Steventon in 1821 shows the Rectory near the road junction. The numbered fields are those farmed by George Austen to supplement his stipend.

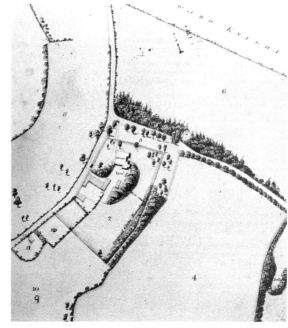

own children had arrived: Henry, Cassandra and Francis. On the 17 December 1775 George Austen sat at his desk in the bow-windowed study at the back of the Rectory surrounded by his library of over 500 books. He reached for his pen and began a letter to his sister-in-law Mrs Walters.

'Last night the time came, and without a great deal of warning, everything was soon happily over. We now have another girl, a present plaything for her sister Cassy and a future companion. She is to be Jenny…'

Throughout all this time George was continually extending the late seventeenth-century dwelling which eventually had five rooms on the ground floor, seven bedrooms and three attics. The surroundings were quiet but the Rectory was always bustling with activity. In 1779 the Austen's eighth and final child was born and christened Charles. With family, boarders and servants, the house was always crowded and Jane was to share a bedroom with her sister for the twenty-five years she lived there.

The Austens were a downwardly mobile branch of an upper middle-class family. George farmed the glebe land around the Rectory to supplement his stipend. Indeed his letter to Mrs Walters went on to talk of the prospects of a ploughing match he was interested in between Kent and Hampshire for a rump of beef, weather permitting.

Cassandra Leigh, Jane's mother, supervised the running of the busy home and the dairy and poultry side of the smallholding farm.

He, like many other village rectors in remote country parishes, was as dependent on the income from his small-holding farm as he was from his clerical living. Jane's mother shared the responsibilities; keeping poultry, growing potatoes and running the dairy. Cheerful and optimistic like her husband, Mrs Austen lacked formal education but had a homespun wit. For thirty years she managed the Steventon domestic situation competently and energetically.

George Austen's study window looked out on a formal garden and turf walk, a sundial, strawberry beds and the grassy bank you can see in the photograph. Looking at the bank one wonders how much of the character of the ten year old Catherine Morland in Jane's *Northanger Abbey* can be attributed to the author herself.

'…she had neither a bad heart nor a bad temper, was seldom stubborn, scarcely ever quarrelsome, and very kind to the little ones, with few interruptions of tyranny; she was moreover noisy and wild, hated confinement and cleanliness, and loved nothing so well in the world as rolling down the green slope at the back of the house.'

'At fifteen, appearances were mending; she began to curl her hair and long for balls; her complexion improved, her features were softened by plumpness and colour, her eyes gained more animation, and her figure more consequence. Her love of dirt gave way to an inclination for finery, and she grew clean as she grew smart; she had now the pleasure of sometimes hearing her father and mother remark on her personal improvement. "Catherine grows quite a good-looking girl – she is almost pretty today".'

To the side of the house there were farm buildings (shown on the map) including the barn used for private family theatricals which took place in 1782 and 1784. Jane's brothers, James and Henry, were the main instigators with James writing the prologues and epilogues for the plays they performed. Jane was seven years old when these theatricals began but she was becoming a teenager when more elaborate productions were staged (possibly inside the house) in 1787 and 1788.

Eliza de Feuillide who caused a sensation by her arrival in the Steventon family circle.

These involved her sophisticated worldly cousin Eliza de Feuillide who had arrived from France in 1786. Eliza, who described herself as the 'outlandish cousin', made quite an impression on the young Jane. It is thought that Jane may have based the character of Mary Crawford from *Mansfield Park* on Eliza. Eliza's French husband, Jean-François Capot de Feuillide was arrested for conspiracy during the revolution and guillotined in 1794. When at Steventon, Eliza flirted outrageously with Jane's brothers James and Henry. She eventually married Henry in December 1797.

In 1801 George Austen decided to leave Steventon and retire to Bath. His eldest son James moved into the Rectory and acted as his father's curate. When George died in 1805, James took over as rector to be followed a decade later by his younger brother Henry who had taken Holy Orders late in life following the collapse of his banking partnership. Henry stayed for only three years, handing over in 1823 to his nephew William Knight.

By this time the old Rectory had become almost uninhabitable. On two occasions, during times of melting snows, the whole ground floor had completely flooded forcing the inhabitants to live upstairs. Edward (Austen) Knight, William's father, built a totally new Rectory for his son standing in 56 acres of additional glebe land on the opposite hillside. When this was complete the old Rectory, with all its memories, along with several nearby cottages was demolished.

Jane had spent the first twenty-five years of her life in Steventon and her letters tell of a very full social life visiting friends at their homes in the neighbourhood – frequently and happily walking many miles to do so. In addition to attending parties in some of the larger houses she regularly went to balls in Basingstoke at the Assembly Rooms and her socializing provided her with much of the material for her novels.

It was here at Steventon, whilst still a teenager, Jane wrote the first drafts of *Elinor & Marianne* which became *Sense & Sensibility*. She began work on a second novel *First Impressions*, in 1796 and completed the initial draft in August 1797 when she was only twenty-one. This was later to become *Pride & Prejudice*. During the middle of 1798, after finishing revisions of *Elinor & Marianne*, Jane began writing a third novel with the working title *Susan*. We know it today as *Northanger Abbey*.

Three-quarters of a mile up the lane by the side of the former rectory is Steventon Manor. For centuries various manor houses stood on or near this site opposite the church. The present building dates from about 2000.

The Steventon estate was owned by the Knight family, distant cousins of George Austen. Two brothers, Hugh and Richard Digweed, rented the estate from the Knights and took possession of the manor house in the summer of 1758. The Digweeds and the Austens became good friends and several members of the Digweed family are mentioned in Jane's letters.

Opposite Steventon Manor is the twelfth-century St Nicholas church where Jane worshipped and where, over time, various members of the Austen family were rectors. In the summer, when the ground was drier underfoot, the family made use of a private footpath which led through the Rectory grounds up to the church.

The twelfth-century church of St Nicholas, where Jane worshipped and where, over time, various members of the Austen family were rectors.

Apart from the replacement steeple, St Nicholas remains essentially unaltered by Victorian restoration and is still much the same as when Jane Austen knew it.

Steventon New Rectory was built in the mid 1820s on high ground overlooking the original site which was prone to flooding.

There are many Austen and Digweed graves in the churchyard including this of James Austen and his second wife Mary Lloyd.

Inside the church are memorials to members of Jane Austen's family; her grandmother Mrs Jane Leigh, her eldest brother James and his two wives; Anne Mathew and Mary Lloyd. There is also a memorial to William Knight and his three little daughters who died in a scarlet fever epidemic in 1848.

Among the many family weddings, christenings and funeral services that took place in the church was that of the marriage of Anna Austen to Benjamin Lefroy on the 8 November 1814. Benjamin Lefroy was the youngest son of Jane Austen's great friend, Mrs Anne Lefroy and her husband, the Reverend George Lefroy of the nearby village of Ashe. Anna was the daughter of James Austen and his first wife, Anne Mathews. Anna's younger half-sister Caroline remembered the wedding in her *Reminiscences*:

This watercolour of Jane was painted by her sister Cassandra.

'Weddings were then usually very quiet. The old fashion of festivity and publicity had quite gone by and was universally condemned as showing the great bad taste of al *(sic)* former generations...My sister's wedding was certainly in the extreme of quietness; yet not so as to be in any way censured or remarked upon – and this was the order of the day.'

'The Bridegroom came from Ashe Rectory where he had hitherto lived with his brother, and Mr. and Mrs. Lefroy came with him, and another brother, Mr. Edward Lefroy. Anne Lefroy, the eldest little girl was one of the bridesmaids and I was the other...We in the house had a slight early breakfast upstairs; and between 9 and 10 the bride, my mother, Mrs. Lefroy, Anne and myself were taken to church in our carriage. All the gentlemen walked...Mr. Lefroy read the service, my father gave his daughter away... I and Anne Lefroy, nine and six years old, wore white frocks and had white ribband *(sic)* on our straw bonnets which I suppose were new for the occasion.'

This interesting account of the quiet wedding celebrations that were common at the time has echoes of the weddings in Jane's novel *Emma* when poor Miss Taylor marries Mr Weston and Emma Woodhouse herself marries Mr Knightley.

Ashe

Anne Lefroy, known as Madam Lefroy, became a friend and mentor to Jane.

Tom Lefroy, Anne Lefroy's nephew, with whom Jane had a brief flirtation.

WHEN GREAT UNCLE Francis Austen gifted the living of Deane to his nephew George Austen, Jane's father, he also sold his assets in the neighbouring village of Ashe to the wealthy Benjamin Langlois. Ten years later, in 1783, Langlois rewarded his own nephew, the Reverend Isaac Peter George Lefroy (known as George Lefroy), by presenting him with the living at Ashe.

On taking up his clerical appointment, Revd George Lefroy and his wife Anne moved into the parsonage, now known as Ashe House. Anne, who was attractive and cultivated, loved entertaining. She soon became hostess to the neighbourhood and was known affectionately and respectfully as 'Madam' Lefroy. Within the Austen's social circle the Lefroy's were their nearest neighbours.

Anne opened a school in the parsonage for the local poor children and taught them to read. She also personally vaccinated hundreds of people in her husband's parish against smallpox. In another act of kindness and generosity Anne would often lend the Lefroy carriage to less affluent families like the Austens.

Anne was twenty-six years older than Jane and had six children but despite the disparity, Jane formed a lasting friendship with her that was established on mutual intelligence and respect. Ashe is 2 miles north of Steventon and located north-west of Ashe Park. It is within reasonable walking distance from Jane's home at Steventon and her visits to the parsonage were frequent. Through a mutual love of literature, the two friends began long discussions about novels, poetry and plays and Jane was given free rein of the parsonage library.

Jane attended many parties and dances in this graceful Georgian house; some of which promised romance. The essential space for partying at Ashe parsonage was created when the dividing doors between the dining-room and morning-room were opened wide.

Anne Lefroy, with the best of intentions, seems to have intervened in Jane's relationships with potential suitors. Her Irish nephew Tom, met Jane at balls held at Deane House and Manydown, then here at Ashe, where Jane flirted and later joked with her sister that she

expected to 'receive an offer' (of marriage) from him. However, Tom was the only son in a family of girls and there was considerable pressure, originating no doubt from old Uncle Benjamin Langlois, for him to marry a woman of wealth. In the event Tom returned home unattached. Much later he became Lord Chief Justice of Ireland. Jane's brief acquaintance with Tom was romanticized in the 2007 film 'Becoming Jane'.

In 1797, perhaps by way of making amends, Anne Lefroy attempted a spot of match-making, inviting a Fellow of Emmanuel College Cambridge to stay at Ashe. The boisterous Revd Samuel Blackall from Devonshire, who Jane afterwards referred to as 'a piece of Perfection, noisy Perfection', was about to be appointed to a parish, and would have needed a wife. Looking back in her middle age, Cassandra referred to him as 'their youthful hero'.

Jane attended many parties and dances in this graceful Georgian house; some of which promised romance. It ceased to be a parsonage in 1905.

The nave of Ashe church contains a faithful reproduction of the fifteenth-century chancel screen that Jane would have known.

The Victorian carpenters tribute to the robin that made her wood-shaving nest on the screen whilst the building work commenced.

Right: Holy Trinity church at Ashe was rebuilt sixty years after Jane's death by the prolific Victorian church architect George Gilbert Scott.

However, in 1798, when Samuel was again invited to Ashe, he declined. He made some lame excuses in a letter sent to Anne Lefroy which she read to Jane. Afterwards Jane commented: 'Mrs Lefroy made no remarks on the letter, nor did she indeed say anything about him as relative to me. Perhaps she thinks she has said too much already.'

On Jane's twenty-ninth birthday, when she was living in Bath, Anne Lefroy was thrown from her horse on Overton Hill and died a few hours later. Four years on, still grieving at the loss, Jane wrote a poem in tribute to the woman she considered one of her closest friends. It included the lines: '…genuine warmth of heart without pretence, And purity of mind that crowns the whole.'

A few steps down the lane from Ashe house is the new Holy Trinity church. This is not the building Jane would have known but the Lefroy graves are here and their monuments have been preserved inside the church. Major rebuilding was carried out between 1878 and 1879 by the prolific Victorian church architect George Gilbert Scott.

The chancel screen is a faithful reproduction of the fifteenth-century original which Jane would have known. While the building work was in progress a robin built a nest of wood shavings on top of the screen. In the wall on the west side of the screen is a small square iron door which opens to reveal a carving of a robin on a nest – a delightful tribute to the little bird that became a source of interest and amusement for the carpenters.

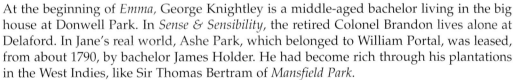

Left: As you approach the main door of Holy Trinity church the Lefroy graves are on the right. Lefroy memorials have been preserved inside the church.

Above: The grave of Captain Robert Portal is at the eastern corner of the churchyard, marked by a white marble cross.
He is a descendant of the Portals of Ashe Park and a survivor of the Charge of the Light Brigade.

At the beginning of *Emma*, George Knightley is a middle-aged bachelor living in the big house at Donwell Park. In *Sense & Sensibility*, the retired Colonel Brandon lives alone at Delaford. In Jane's real world, Ashe Park, which belonged to William Portal, was leased, from about 1790, by bachelor James Holder. He had become rich through his plantations in the West Indies, like Sir Thomas Bertram of *Mansfield Park*.

The Austens were often invited to the Park and there are many references in Jane's letters to friends and neighbours being present at card-playing and dinner parties of fourteen. There are also a couple of references to Mr Holder that seem to be at odds. In the first, written in 1800 she says: 'To sit in idleness over a good fire in a well-proportioned room is a luxurious sensation. Sometimes we talked and sometimes we were quite silent. I said two or three amusing things, and Mr Holder made a few infamous puns.'

A year later, in a letter written from Steventon on Sunday 25 January 1801 she is reporting to Cassandra: 'Your unfortunate sister was betrayed last Thursday into a situation of the

The Austens were often invited to Ashe Park and there are many references in Jane's letters to friends and neighbours being present at card-playing and dinner parties of fourteen.

utmost cruelty. I arrived at Ashe Park before the party from Deane, and was shut up in the drawing-room with Mr Holder alone for ten minutes. I had some thoughts of insisting on the housekeeper or Mary Corbett being sent for, and nothing could prevail on me to move two steps from the door, on the lock of which I kept one hand constantly fixed. We met nobody but ourselves, played at vingt-un again, and were very cross'.

Two thirds of the present house at Ashe Park is a Victorian reconstruction. A recent Estate Agent's advertisement listed it as: 'A classic seven-bedroom Georgian brick house with three cottages, stabling, 235 acres, and a long, tree-lined carriage drive. It also has a swimming pool, tennis court, farm buildings and a polo ground.' The extensive gardens within the grounds of the estate are open each spring under the National Gardens Scheme.

Two-thirds of the present house at Ashe Park is a Victorian reconstruction. The 'well-proportioned' room Jane admired is now incorporated into the present dining room.

Oakley

THE VILLAGE OF Oakley was on Jane's route from Deane Gate to the major town of Basingstoke, along the road we now know as the A3400. She was frequently making her way in this direction, usually walking and often accompanied by Cassandra, to visit the Bramstons at Oakley Hall but more especially the Wither sisters at Manydown.

Today Oakley Hall is a smart hotel and a good base from which to explore Jane Austen country. Wither Bramston, who was contemporary with Jane's parents, demolished an older building on the site where novelist Henry Fielding had stayed on several occasions. Wither completed the new Oakley Hall in 1795 after his marriage to Miss Mary Chute of The Vyne, Sherborne St John, north of Basingstoke.

The oak bar, on the right, has been installed in the main reception room.

In 1860 an additional storey and the 'porte-cochère' were added to the Hall that Jane knew.

During the time Oakley Hall was used as a college this library was the headmaster's study. Former pupils visiting the hotel as guests are amused at the privilege of having access to this inner sanctum.

Opposite: The patio overlooks the garden and grounds where Jane was free to wander.

The building we see today is not exactly as Jane would have known it. In 1860, a second storey and the 'porte-cochère' were added. This type of 'carriage porch' was designed so a horse and carriage could pass through it in order for the occupants to alight under cover, protected from the weather.

The Austens socialized with the Bramstons and Jane mentions them and the house in a number of her letters including this one, written to Cassandra on 25 October 1800: 'On Thursday we walked to Deane, yesterday to Oakley Hall and Oakley, and to-day to Deane again. At Oakley we did a great deal – ate some sandwiches all over mustard, admired Mr. Bramston's porter, and Mrs. Bramston's transparencies, and gained a promise from the latter of two roots of heartsease, one all yellow, the other all purple, for you.'

It is thought by some that Jane drew inspiration for the character of Lady Bertram in *Mansfield Park* from Mrs Bramston. *Lady Bertram* is consistently depicted reclining on the sofa with her pug dog. She is often dozing and has a general air of laudanum-induced indolence and yet the other family members defer to her and absolve her of responsibilities.

After reading *Mansfield Park*, Mrs Bramston actually commented with good humour and wit about the similarity and Jane recorded Mrs B's reaction: '...much pleased with it; particularly with the character of Fanny, as being so very natural. Thought Lady Bertram like herself. Preferred it to either of the others—but imagined THAT might be her want of Taste—as she does not understand Wit.'

Mrs Bramston had a taste for Gothic novels and it is possible she lent copies to Jane. To Jane's obvious amusement, Wither Bramston's eccentric sister Augusta commented on her novels and: 'owned that she thought S&S and P&P downright nonsense, but expected to find MP better, & having finished the 1st vol.—flattered herself she had got through the worst.'

Jane comments that she visited 'Oakley Hall and Oakley'. At the time, Oakley Village had a haberdashery shop where the Austens probably had an account. In the same letter of 25 October we see how a parson's daughter considered the welfare of the poor of the parish: 'At Oakley we bought ten pair of worsted stockings and a shift; the shift is for Betty Dawkins, as we find she wants it more than a rug; she is one of the most grateful of all whom Edward's charity has reached, or at least she expresses herself more warmly than the rest, for she sends him a "sight of thanks".'

In 1940 Oakley Hall became home to Hilsea College, for boarding naval officers' children relocated to avoid air raids over Portsmouth during the Second World War. From 1992 the Hall began moving into a new phase of life, firstly as a conference centre and eventually being beautifully restored to its former self and opening as a hotel with eighteen luxurious bedrooms.

Opposite: In the centre of the village a number of old cottages remain which Jane would have known.

Manydown, Wootton & Worting

THE ESTATE OF Manydown was located 2½ miles west of Basingstoke, between Oakley and Worting just south of the village of Wootton St Lawrence. Here we look in vain for traces of the house that featured so largely in Jane Austen's life. It was at Manydown in January 1796 that Jane first flirted with Tom Lefroy and joked in a letter to Cassandra about her shocking behaviour:

'I am almost afraid to tell you how my Irish friend and I behaved. Imagine to yourself everything most profligate and shocking in the way of dancing and sitting down together. I can expose myself however, only *once more*, because he leaves the country soon after next Friday, on which day we *are* to have a dance at Ashe after all.'

In 1796, following the flirtation with Tom Lefroy, Jane began work on *First Impressions* which was later published as *Pride & Prejudice*. In the novel our heart goes out to Charlotte Lucas, Elizabeth Bennet's friend. Fearing of becoming a burden to her family, Charlotte makes an economic decision, and agrees to marry the ridiculous Reverend Collins, heir to Longbourn.

Harris Bigg-Wither was the last man with whom Jane is known to have been emotionally involved, and the only man definitely known to have made her a proposal of marriage.

Four years after writing the story Jane found herself in a not dissimilar situation. Jane and Cassandra were living in Bath with their mother when they took a trip to North Hampshire to visit old friends. It was in December 1802, when Jane was approaching her twenty-seventh birthday. She was still unattached when she had a proposal of marriage from twenty-one year old Harris Bigg-Wither, heir to the Manydown estate.

Harris's father, Lovelace Bigg, inherited the property from cousins who were called Wither, so he decided to change his name to Bigg-Wither and changed his sons' names also. Confusingly the daughters kept their surname of Bigg.

Three of Harris's nine sisters, Alethea, Catherine and Elizabeth were among the Austen girls' most intimate friends and Jane and Cassandra were regular visitors to Manydown, often staying the night after attending the Basingstoke balls. On the night of the proposal Jane and Cassandra were staying with Alethea, Catherine and their married sister

A print of Manydown made in Jane's day.

Left: This photograph was taken in 1965 shortly before Manydown was demolished.

Elizabeth, who had returned to the family home after the death of her husband William Heathcote.

The Bigg sisters could see advantages for themselves if Jane became their sister-in-law; particularly as they might be able to stay on at Manydown after their father's death when Harris would inherit. They may well have encouraged their brother to make the proposal; they could also appreciate the advantages for their friend Jane in becoming the mistress of Manydown Park. Jane would have been aware of the financial advantages for herself and the opportunity it would present in allowing her to provide for both Cassandra and her parents.

Although his portrait might suggest otherwise, Harris was by some accounts rather ungainly and awkward with an unfortunate stammer. A month before the proposal, Jane mentioned Harris in a letter: 'Harris seems still in a poor way, from his bad habit of body; his hand bled again a little the other day and Dr Littlehales has been with him lately.' We shall probably never know what his 'bad habit of body' was but it may have been psoriasis.

Given Harris's problems it is all the more surprising that Jane accepted the proposal in the first place. However, the general rejoicing in the household was short lived because she revoked her decision the following morning. The occasion was filled with emotion. Jane must have dwelt all night on the disadvantages of the union.

She hurriedly left the house the next morning and fled to Steventon where she forcefully persuaded her brother James to take her and Cassandra back to Bath the next day. She refused to tell James or his wife Mary what the trouble was. Harris was the last man with whom Jane is known to have been emotionally involved, and the only man definitely known to have made her a proposal of marriage.

Two years after the debacle, Harris married Anne Howe-Frith, daughter of a North Hampshire militia lieutenant-colonel. They lived in Quidhampton and Wymering and went on to have 10 children. Harris did not return to Manydown until after his father's death in 1813 when he inherited the estate.

The main section of the house was eighteenth-century but the earlier part dated to the fourteenth. By the 1960s it had become impossible to maintain. In 1965, when the family failed to sell it, or even give it away, it was proposed to pull it down.

There was an outcry from 'Janeites' because it was unthinkable to destroy a place of which

Wootton St Lawrence Church where Jane worshipped contains many memorials to the Bigg-Wither family including one to Harris Bigg-Wither.

Charles Slegg Ward, vicar here from 1876 to 1908 was grandfather of poet and artist Laurence Whistler who produced this beautiful engraving of Manydown House on one of the church windows.

Worting House was owned by Lovelace Bigg-Wither, during Jane's time and rented by her friends John and Anne Clarke.

Jane Austen might have become chatelaine. But as nobody came forward with the money for its restoration, it was demolished. All we are left with today are old prints and photographs and a few tantalizing hints at what went on there.

Jane was known to have stayed at Manydown over some weekends and would therefore have, on occasion, worshipped with the Bigg-Wither family at their parish church of Wootton St Lawrence. The church was restored in 1864 and certain medieval features that Jane would have known, including the Norman doorway, have been preserved.

Continuing east along the B3400 towards Basingstoke we immediately enter Worting. In 1797, Lovelace Bigg-Wither purchased this adjoining estate with its eighteenth-century house. He let the house to John Clarke who had married Anne, daughter of Carew Mildmay of Shawford near Winchester.

On Thursday 20 December 1798, the twenty-three year old Jane Austen was staying at Manydown with her friend Catherine Bigg, in anticipation of attending the monthly ball at the Basingstoke Assembly Rooms. The girls were in need of a chaperone and called on Mrs Clarke. Jane mentions the event in a letter to Cassandra dated 24 December, from which we can believe there were probably other unrecorded visits to Worting House:

'I spent my time very quietly and pleasantly with Catherine. Miss Blachford (a cousin of the Biggs, also a guest in the house) is agreeable enough. I do not want people to be very agreeable as it saves me the trouble of liking them a great deal. I found only Catherine and her when I got to Manydown on Thursday. We dined together and went together to Worting to seek the protection of Mrs Clarke…'

The Clarkes are mentioned in a number of letters as being present at several of the Assembly balls. We are also told that Mr Clarke was an admirer of the poet William Cowper, Jane's favourite poetical moralist. On an occasion at Ashe Park we hear that Mrs Bramston of Oakley Hall talked a great deal of nonsense which Mr Bramston and Mr Clarke seemed equally to enjoy. 'There was a whist and a casino table and six outsiders.'

Worting House is a Grade II-listed building. It was converted in 1988 for commercial use and now provides office space for more than 30 local firms, with additional services including desk space by the hour, training and meeting rooms, and call-handling. What would Jane make of that I wonder?

The Grade II-listed building was converted in 1988 for commercial use and now provides office space for more than 30 local firms.

Basingstoke

Now a pedestrian precinct, London Street and Winchester Street meet in the old Market Place.

FOLLOWING IN JANE'S steps, we continue east along the B3400 heading into the suburbs of Basingstoke. The small market town which Jane knew has grown forty fold in population and area, swallowing up parishes, farms and country estates. The western extremity of the conurbation now abuts the boundary of Worting.

From here we pass through commercial and retail developments, searching for what remains of the old town and traces of locations that Jane would have known. They can still be found along the pedestrianised section of the old coaching road to London which passes right through the Market Place, also in Church Road which leads down from the Market Place to the river crossing. Although the River Loddon is now only a very small stream, in the past it had a considerable flow and its water was used in various industrial processes such as fulling cloth, milling and brewing.

The main attraction of Basingstoke for Jane was the monthly balls. These were usually held on a Thursday during the winter in the Assembly Rooms above the old Town Hall. Well-to-do families from the outlying neighbourhood travelled long distances to attend these gatherings, undeterred by the dangers of dark winter nights, lampless lanes and stormy weather. Jane's early letters are full of references to the people of her acquaintance who were present.

We learn of John Chute (from The Vyne at Sherborne St John), Lord Portsmouth (from Hurstbourne Park), Lord Dorchester (from Kempshott Park) and Lord Bolton (from Hackwood) who were all together on an evening when there where thirty couples. In a letter of December 1798 Jane tells us: 'There were twenty dances, and I danced them all, and without any fatigue.'

Jane obviously drew on these experiences as material for her novels which are rich in descriptions of balls and etiquette. In *Pride and Prejudice* the Netherfield ball is a pivotal scene in which the dancing between the Bennet girls and their respective suitors reflect the social conventions of the time. Jane used the strict rules of Regency dancing to reflect Elizabeth's feelings for Wickham, Darcy and, reluctantly, Mr Collins.

When this courtship is augmented by a midnight feast, the light of a full moon and the elegant mode of dress, it's hardly surprising that Regency balls like Netherfield have captured the attention of readers from the time of the novel's publication.

Now I need to address a general misconception about the venue for the Basingstoke balls. A plaque on the Barclay's Bank building in the Market Place states: 'Behind here stood the Assembly Rooms where the novelist Jane Austen attended dances.' In Jane's time this site was occupied by the Angel Inn which did have a large room over the stables at the back. This room however would have been used for country dances rather than balls and attended by ordinary working folk and trades people. The aristocratic and middle class frequented the large Assembly Room above the Town Hall which stood opposite, roughly where the TSB Bank stands now.

Constance Hill, in her book *Jane Austen: Her Homes and Her Friends* (1923) made the error of identification. Her enthusiastic account of the discovery, illustrated by her sister's

The misleading plaque is affixed to the Barclay's Bank which occupies the site where the Angel Inn formerly stood. The dance rooms were in a hay loft above the inn's stables and coach house at the rear.

The old Town Hall with the rooms above which could accommodate up to 300 people.

39

exquisite drawings, is very evocative but owes more to romance than research. Subsequent biographers, captivated by the account, have perpetuated the error.

The two principal posting inns at Basingstoke at this time were the Crown and the Maidenhead, where Mrs Martin was the landlady until February 1798. She organised the Basingstoke balls, made all the arrangements and placed notices in the local newspapers. It is clear Mrs Martin was targeting the elite because working people could not afford newspapers.

Between 1792 and 1801 advertisements appeared in the *Reading Mercury* and *Oxford Gazette* for 56 Basingstoke balls. None of these assemblies was held at any of the inns. On 46 of these occasions the Town Hall is specifically mentioned as being the venue.

Mrs Martin was known to Jane. After February 1798, she left the Maidenhead Inn and took over the millinery and haberdashery business of Mr John Chambers in Basingstoke where Jane must have shopped. On the 14 January 1799, Mrs Martin also opened a circulating library and informed Jane of the initiative:

'I have received a very civil note from Mrs Martin requesting my name as a Subscriber to her Library ... As an inducement to subscribe Mrs Martin tells us that her Collection is not to consist only of Novels, but of every kind of Literature &c &c – She might have spared this pretension to our family, who are great Novel-readers & not ashamed of being so.'

The Maidenhead Inn was taken over by Willliam Wilson who was also landlord of the Crown and from March 1798 the assembly balls were organised by him. A few steps west along Winchester Street from the Market Place is a rather sad looking building which is now home to a number of retail businesses, primarily The Basingstoke Service Centre. This is what is left of the once proud Crown Inn. The arched opening bearing the name Joice's Yard was formerly the entrance to the coach-yard and stables.

On Saturday 6 September 1782, John Byng, Viscount Torrington, stayed here and had this to say about the Crown: 'Having arrived in Basingstoke I found an inn of good fare, and had a sole and a rabbit for supper. The wheat is all housed, but the barley is not yet ripe enough for cutting; which is a great preservative of the game. As usual I took a short evening walk.' The following day Byng, who is not generally known for his compliments says: 'The inn of last night I may praise for its good larder, good stabling, and good beds.'

In Jane's time many of the distinguished local gentlemen she knew attended a dining club here. The North Hants Club met at the Crown and hosted a grand annual ball at the Town

Jane would have been very familiar with this the type of cloakroom scene at an Assembly ball.

Hall Assembly Rooms. Following dinner at the inn, club members would play whist and discuss business. One of the frequent topics was the Basingstoke Canal Company of which most of the members held shares. Perhaps Jane had the Basingstoke Crown in mind when in *Emma* she had Frank Churchill observe of the Crown Inn at Hartfield: '… the highest purpose for which it was ever wanted was to accommodate a whist club established among the gentlemen and half-gentlemen of the place.'

With the advent of train travel the Crown, like the majority of the old coaching inns, became unsustainable. In 1840 the landlady of that time went bankrupt. An advertisement in the *Reading Mercury* of 19 September 1840 listed items to be sold at auction which included: '21 post horses, four mules, two cows in calf, 15 pigs, post chaises, flys, mourning coaches, 170 dozen bottles of port and sherry wines, 300 ounces of plate, brewing plant, 2,000 gallons of beer, the furniture of 30 rooms, 27 bedsteads, 27 feather beds, mattresses and bedding, mahogany furniture, linen, carpets, china and glass.'

By 1880 the Crown had been reduced to a small tavern. John Joice, who had established a coach and carriage building business in the yard, expanded his enterprise into the warren of outbuildings formerly owned by the inn.

This ancient coaching arch, once part of the Crown, leads through to the area where John Joice had his coach-building business located in the former outbuildings of the inn.

As I write, the former Crown Inn is leaning for support against the building next door.

Part of the display of everyday articles used by the Austen family two-hundred years ago displayed at the Willis Museum.

Left: The later Town Hall is now home to the Willis Museum and houses a small exhibition of artifacts recovered during an archeological dig in 2011 at the site of Steventon Rectory.

One inn that Jane would have known remains and thrives, this is the Red Lion. Stage-coaches the Austens travelled in on round trips to Kent, would have stopped here. In October 1798, on a journey back from Godmersham, Mrs Austen was fortified by a night stop at Staines and a 'mess of broth' at Basingstoke. This may well have been at the Red Lion, which is situated at the London end of the present day precinct and has the best preserved façade of the remaining old inn buildings.

In 1840 a new Town Hall was built adjacent to the site of the original. It is now home to the Willis Museum which houses a small exhibition of artifacts recovered during an archeological dig in 2011 at the site of Steventon Rectory.

Church Street leads down by the side of the Willis Museum. After their marriage, Reverend George Lefroy and his wife Anne lived in a house in Church Street and attended

The Red Lion has the best preserved façade of the large number of inns that once flanked both sides of this important highway. Charles Dickens featured this inn as the Bald Faced Stag in his novel *Martin Chuzzlewit*.

St Michael's Church. Although George does not appear to have had any official position in the church, he did attend vestry meetings.

There is a memorial in St Michael's church to the Lefroy's baby daughter Julia Elizabeth who survived only a few weeks. There is also a tablet to George's mother, Elizabeth, who came to live near them in Church Street. Despite being dismissed by Thomas Hardy in his 1895 novel *Jude the Obscure* as gaunt and unattractive, St Michael's is a Grade I-listed building, largely of sixteenth-century construction in stone and flint.

Revd George Austen and other members of the family purchased items from John Ring who had a cabinet making and upholstery business in Church Street. John and his sons had several workshops in the area. It is likely that the main premises and family home was the handsome house at the most northerly end of the surviving row of houses before you reach Chute House. It is now occupied by Office Angels.

Jane's father is thought to have purchased her small walnut writing table from Rings and her treasured mahogany writing box in which she kept her paper, pens and ink. The box, which opens to provide a writing slope, is now in the British Library.

Despite being dismissed by Thomas Hardy in *Jude the Obscure* as 'gaunt and unattractive', St Michael's church is a Grade I-listed building.

The Church Street family home and business premises of John Ring and Sons, cabinet makers and upholsterers, where the Austens were valued customers.

Sherborne St John & The Vyne

THE VYNE, NORTH of Basingstoke, in the parish of Sherborne St John, is a beautiful Tudor house built between 1500 and 1520 for William, Lord Sandys, Lord Chamberlain to Henry VIII. The house later passed to the Chute family who in 1956 bequeathed it along with 1124 acres to the National Trust. Among the highlights are a superb Tudor chapel and an ornately decorated Palladian staircase, as well as the striking neo-classical portico which is one of the earliest in England.

The Vyne is a beautiful Tudor house built between 1500 and 1520 for William, Lord Sandys, Lord Chamberlain to Henry VIII.

In Jane's time the property was owned by William John Chute who was Master of the Vyne Hunt and MP for Hampshire. When William inherited the estate from his father in 1790, he was thirty-three, single and in possession of a good fortune; so naturally it was

Above right: The extraordinary ice-cool Palladian Staircase Hall is one of the most striking features of the house.

Above left: When impromptu dancing followed a dinner party it would have taken place in one of the drawing rooms with the furniture moved aside and the carpet rolled back.

universally accepted that he was in want of a wife. Jane was not a contender; she was just fourteen at the time but she must have picked up on the speculation among the chattering Hampshire ladies about whom he might choose.

Jane's eldest brother James was always a keen huntsman. When he lived at Deane he rode out with the Vyne Hunt and became friendly with William Chute who, in 1791, presented him to the living of Sherborne St John. This was a position James was to hold jointly with that of Steventon (from 1805) until his death in 1819.

In 1793 William finally put an end to the Hampshire neighbourhood's speculation by marrying Eliza Smith, one of the daughters of Devizes MP Joshua Smith. On many occasions, after taking the Sunday service at St Andrew's church in the village, James Austen would ride over and have dinner at The Vyne with William and Eliza, often taking his son James Edward with him.

St Andrew's church in the village of Sherborne St John where James Austen, Jane's oldest brother, held the living from 1791 until his death in 1815.

James Edward Austen, seen here in later life, married Mrs Chute's niece Emma Smith. He went on to write the first biography of his beloved Aunt Jane.

Jane did not seem to care much for William. On Friday 15 January 1796, she wrote to Cassandra, from Steventon: 'Wm. Chute called here yesterday. I wonder what he means by being so civil. There is a report that Tom is going to be married to a Litchfield Lass.'

The 'Tom' Jane refers to is William's younger brother, Thomas Vere Chute who was just three years older than Jane. Tom, who remained a bachelor all his life, lived on the family estate in Norfolk. He visited The Vyne for three months each year during the hunting season bringing his three favourite horses with him. Jane mentions dancing with him at the Basingstoke Assemblies.

Revd and Mrs Austen accompanied by Cassandra were occasional visitors to The Vyne. But on Tuesday 26 March 1799, Eliza recorded in her journal that Jane was with them and they dined together with Mr Digweed. Jane seemed to be rather lukewarm about Eliza. It has been suggested that she might have been jealous of the time her particular friends, Alethea and Catherine Bigg from Manydown, spent in the company of Eliza.

On 25 October 1800 Jane recorded: 'This morning we called at the Harwoods, and in their dining-room found "Heathcote and Chute for ever" – Mrs. William Heathcote and Mrs Chute – the first of whom took a long ride yesterday morning with Mrs. Harwood into Lord Carnarvon's park, and fainted away in the evening, and the second walked down from Oakley Hall attended by Mrs Augusta Bramston; they had meant to come on to Steventon afterwards, but we knew a trick worth two of that.'

The mention of "Heathcote and Chute for ever" was a reference to the joint slogan the two Hampshire MPs used during their political campaigning. Mrs William Heathcote was Elizabeth, the married sister of Alethea and Catherine Bigg. From this it seems clear that Jane was not on the same terms with the older sister.

From other entries in Eliza Chute's journal we learn that she led a lonely life at the great house. When William wasn't away in London he was invariably out hunting. The couple lived for ten years without having children before adopting three-year-old Caroline Wiggett in 1803. Caroline was the daughter of William's cousin whose wife had died leaving a large family. Ten years later, when Jane was writing *Mansfield Park*, she created the character of Fanny Price whose life has parallels with that of Caroline.

There are also vague indications that Jane danced at The Vyne but not in the famous Tudor long gallery. We know from the journal of Caroline Wiggett, that the gallery was used as both a lumber room and her playroom and Eliza had partly turned it into a conservatory. Caroline confirms home life at The Vyne was generally quiet and uneventful. The Chutes gave only two or three dinner parties a year and, if impromptu dancing followed, it would have been in one of the drawing rooms with the furniture moved aside and the carpet rolled back.

During visits to The Vyne, James Edward met the Chute's niece Emma Smith, whom he eventually married in 1828. Known as Edward in the family, James Edward was Jane's favourite nephew. She once said of him: 'his Aunts … love him better & better, as they see the sweet temper & warm affections of the Boy confirmed in the young Man.' James Edward was to become his aunt Jane's first biographer. Like his grandfather and father before him he took Holy Orders but spent most of his clerical life in Hertfordshire.

Two things strike today's visitors to The Vyne. The Tudor origins have bequeathed relatively small rooms for such a large house. Secondly, subsequent Chute owners redecorated parts of the interior to the fashionable style of their time. This means that as you pass through the house you move from one period to another with bewildering frequency.

The Chute family bequeathed The Vyne to the National Trust in 1956.

North Waltham & Kempshott

THE LANE LEADING south from Steventon passes through the village of North Waltham before reaching a junction with the old Winchester to Basingstoke Road. This area is known as Popham Lane and the old road which passes in front of the Wheatsheaf Inn was originally built by the Romans. By the time of the Austens' residence in the area it had become part of the important coaching route linking Southampton to London, roughly following the line of the present-day M3 motorway.

On 7 August 1792, Jane's cousin, Jane Cooper stayed at the Wheatsheaf with her family and the following morning the Austens joined them there for breakfast. In December 1793 Jane and Cassandra waited at the inn with their luggage and their older sailor brother Francis to catch a coach to Southampton. Frank was home on leave and able to escort his sisters on a trip to spend Christmas with their cousins the Butler-Harrisons who lived in Southampton.

The village pond and thatched cottages of North Waltham so familiar to Jane on her walks to Popham Lane.

Members of the Austen family would often walk from the rectory to the inn to collect their mail. In her memoir of her aunt, Caroline Austen provides us with a vivid picture of Jane and Cassandra with bonnets tied tight and cloaks fastened at the neck, undertaking just such an errand:

'I recollect how they walked in wintry weather through the sloppy lane… in pattens usually worn at that time even by Gentlewomen. I remember too their bonnets; because precisely alike in colour, shape and material, I made it a pleasure to guess, & I believed always guessed right, which bonnet & which aunt belonged to each other.'

The pattens that Caroline mentions were clog-like overshoes, with iron rings beneath their wooden soles, which raised the wearer several inches above the muddy rutted ground.

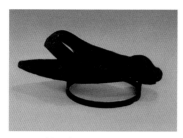

Pattens like these were worn by Jane and Cassandra on their winter walks.

Cassandra's portrait of Jane, this time with her bonnet ribbons untied.

As recipients, the Austens had to pay for their letters, one of which on the 11 February 1801, was from Charles, the younger of the two sailor brothers: 'written last Saturday from off the Start, and conveyed to Popham Lane by Captain Boyle in his way to Midgham.'

Mr Vernon was the proprietor of the Wheatsheaf at the time and a friend of the Austens. He was well acquainted with Jane's eldest brother James, who was a keen huntsman. The Wheatsheaf was a very popular haunt of the hunting fraternity and was the venue for many post-hunt dinners.

Mr Vernon kept a fine cellar of port wine at the inn which was reserved for members of the Hampshire Hunt. Charles Powlett, who attended the dinners at the Wheatsheaf, was the 'poet of the Hampshire Hunt'. He immortalised the role of the landlord and the inn, in a song which was sung at their monthly dinners. It is not difficult to imagine the scene. Here are the lyrics to the first and last verse:

'Draw near, ye frail mortals of every degree / Who heartily sigh and complain / We'll find you a medicine, without any fee / Shall quickly alleviate your pain / Would you drive away care / To the Wheatsheaf repair / Where mirth and good humour embrace / Our Hampshire Hunt join / While young mirth and old wine / Enliven the joys of the chase!'

'On tithes and obligations no longer intent / The parson came hobbling along / To forward the sport ever anxiously bent / Though feeble and last in the throng / his weak muse and his horse / Have alike run their course / Long hacknay'd, exhausted, and lame / Yet the veteran entreats / In return for past feats / Your favour he humbly may claim / Then, to drive away care / He'll to Vernon's repair / Where wit and good humour embrace / The Hampshire Hunt join / With young mirth and old wine / Enliven the joys of the chase.'

Like many Georgian houses, the red-brick façade of the Wheatsheaf hides a much older timber frame building standing on earlier foundations. Modern accommodation wings have been added to the inn and the bar/restaurant is now of the open-plan exposed brick and beam style.

Four miles east of Steventon is Kempshott. In 1788, when Jane was thirteen, the neighbourhood was abuzz with news that the Prince of Wales had taken a lease on the Kempshott Estate in order to pursue his love of stag hunting. Stephen Terry of Dummer rode out with the Prince and his cronies, as did James Austen, who no doubt talked about the goings on when back at the Steventon Rectory.

The Wheatsheaf where the Austens collected their mail was run at the time by Mr Vernon.

Left: The exposed beams and red brick enhance the attractive present day interior of the Wheatsheaf.

Kempshott House where Jane attended dances as a guest of Lord and Lady Dorchester after the Prince of Wales had relinquished the lease.

In 1788, when Jane was thirteen, the neighbourhood was abuzz with news that the Prince of Wales had taken a lease on the Kempshott Estate in order to pursue his love of stag hunting.

However, by 1793 the Prince's profligate life style was catching up with him. He was becoming unfit to ride to hounds and without his patronage, the Kempshott Hunt ceased to exist. In 1795 he married Caroline of Brunswick and the couple spent their honeymoon at Kempshott but his mounting debt crisis meant retrenching all round. After 1795, when the Prince had ceased to visit the area, Mr Vernon went bankrupt. His fine cellar of port wine was seized by his creditors and sold at auction.

In 1796 Sir Guy Carleton, first Baron Dorchester, succeeded the Prince of Wales as the tenant of Kempshott Park and Jane was invited to balls held there. On 28 December 1798, Jane reports to Cassandra:

'There was the same kind of supper as last year, and the same want of chairs. There were more dancers than the room could conveniently hold, which is enough to constitute a good ball at any time.'

Kempshott House was eventually demolished to make way for the M3 motorway but the Old Coach House remains as a reminder of grander days. It has been retained and refurbished for commercial and residential use.

Dummer

DUMMER, WHICH IS about 2½ miles south-east of Steventon, is one of the smallest villages in Hampshire with a present population of under four-hundred. It is located close to Popham Lane and today's visitors have to pass under the M3 Motorway to gain access. For Jane and Cassandra, there were no such obstacles. In good weather, it must have been a delightful walk along the lanes and across the fields.

The Terry family who lived in the small handsome manor house next to the church were friends of the Austens. Thirteen children were born here to the squire and his wife between the mid 1770s and the 1790s and a good many of them are mentioned in Jane's letters.

The small handsome manor house almost hidden behind the church was home to the Terry family.

The eight-hundred year old All Saints' church. Note the little dormer window that lights the gallery.

The chancel arch of All Saints' has a canopy that is very rare in the county.

The ancient pulpit from where George Whitefield preached dates from 1380 and is one of the six oldest pulpits in the country.

All Saints' church has an ancient gallery that covers more than half the depth of the nave.

Of the thirteen children, Stephen and Michael were closest to Jane's age and the other eleven younger. She was often critical of them. As a group she found them noisy but could rely on Stephen, who was just one year older, to partner her at dances. Writing about the Basingstoke ball which took place on Thursday 30 October 1800, Jane says:

'There was a scarcity of Men in general, & a still greater scarcity of any that were good for much. I danced nine dances out of ten, five with Stephen Terry, T. Chute & James Digweed & four with Catherine. There was commonly a couple of ladies standing up together, but not often any so amiable as ourselves.'

The Terrys were not only influential in the history of the parish for almost two centuries they were also part of the vibrant social scene which provided material for Jane as an aspiring novelist. Stephen and Michael might have been considered eligible for the Austen sisters, but it was not to be. Years later, Michael was briefly engaged to Jane's niece Anna; and Anna's daughter subsequently described him as being as stupid as Mr Rushworth from *Mansfield Park* or Mr Collins from *Pride and Prejudice*. Two of the Terry daughters, Jane and Eliza respectively married Harry Digweed and Charles Harwood.

Stephen Terry has left us with a picture of life in the parish during and after Jane's time in his *Diaries of Dummer*. They are mostly concerned with the exploits of the hunting fraternity which included Jane's eldest brother James, a regular guest at Dummer House. Stephen Terry also reveals stories of the excesses of the Prince of Wales which scandalized the neighbourhood during the time he rented nearby Kempshott House.

'The Prince himself... lived hard and drank deep. He was already ungainly and crippled with gout. Nanny Stephens, of Dummer, a stout, strong woman, was deputed to be his nurse and even helped him out of the bath like a baby, while his lazy valet did nothing but brush his clothes and look on.'

The 1861 census shows George Terry living at Dummer Grange while Stephen himself is still alive at the age of eighty-six and farming 450 acres, with 12 men to support his large family in Dummer House and a wet nurse for one of his grandchildren.

All Saints' church, parts of which date to the twelfth-century, has a number of things of particular interest. The queer little dormer window projecting from the southern side of the roof gives light to an ancient gallery which covers more than half the depth of the nave. Set above the chancel arch, and curving round under the nave roof, is a great fifteenth-century wooden canopy. It is decorated with gilded bosses and was designed to form a background to the crucifix on the old rood-loft.

The Old Brewery was active in the days when the village was self-sufficient.

The ancient pulpit with traceried panels is one of the oldest in England. When Jane's father was a boy, George Whitefield was given the curacy here and preached from this pulpit. Whitefield went on to become the most famous religious figure of the eighteenth-century, capable of commanding thousands of listeners on two continents through the sheer power of his oratory. In his lifetime, he preached at least 18,000 times to perhaps 10 million people. Actor David Garrick said of him: 'I would give a hundred guineas, if I could say "Oh" like Mr. Whitefield.'

In Jane's time, Dummer was a thriving village supporting a variety of trades. In addition to the manor house, church and cottages, she would have known the brewery and the forge which are still here, as is the covered village well, with the 10' wheel used for drawing up the water.

The 10' diameter wheel used for drawing water up from the well in Jane's time.

Left: The covered well house that Jane would have known.

Stephen Terry who has given us a picture of life in the parish during and after Jane's time in his *Diaries of Dummer*.

Hackwood

FOUR MILES NORTH-EAST of Dummer village is Hackwood Park. The large country estate lies to the south of Basingstoke; severed from the encroachment of the town suburbs by the thrusting cut of the M3 motorway.

Hackwood was the grandest house which Jane knew in her youth but she was not intimidated or overly impressed by it or its owner. She knew Lord Bolton from his visits to Manydown and the Basingstoke Assemblies but the acquaintance was slight and perhaps unrewarding for, as she implied in this letter of 2 December 1798, he seemed to be less interested in people than he was in his pigs:

Hackwood was the grandest house Jane knew in her youth. The equestrian lead statue of George I was a present from the King to the 3rd Duke of Bolton.

The main lodge gate is just south of the M3 but the house cannot be seen from here.

'Lord Bolton is particularly curious in his pigs, has had pigstyes of a most elegant construction built for them, and visits them every morning as soon as he rises.'

Although Revd George Austen was a modest parson, he was an educated man and related to Thomas Knight, owner of the Steventon Estate. As such Lord Bolton would not think it unusual to invite him and his daughters to his splendid parties. Jane took such entertainments in her stride and as material for her novels. She mentions the 'Hackwood balls' in a letter to Cassandra dated 8 January 1799:

'I am not to wear my white satin cap to-night. after all; I am to wear a mamaluc cap instead, which Charles Fowle sent to Mary, and which she lends me. It is all the fashion now; worn at the opera, and by Lady Mildmays at Hackwood balls. I hate describing such things, and I dare say you will be able to guess what it is like.'

The estate was split up in 1986 into small units and sold off. The house, stable block, three cottages and 160 acres went to one buyer. The present owner is very protective of privacy.

Jane saw an earlier version of Hackwood than we see today. Shortly after her visits the central part of the house was doubled in size creating two great rooms. At the east end of the south front, the ballroom in which she danced, is now an indoor swimming pool.

In 1850 the Boltons decided to leave Hackwood and take up residence at Bolton Hall in Yorkshire. Accordingly, Hackwood House was let with all of its furniture. During the Second World War it was used as a hospital for Canadian soldiers. In 1986 the estate was put up for sale as a whole but failed to attract sufficient interest, perhaps because of the inescapable noise from the motorway. As a result, the contents were sold at auction and the estate split up into small units and sold off. The house, stable block, three cottages and 160 acres went to one buyer.

To the north of the M3 is the Crabtree Plantation which was part of the Hackwood Estate, in Jane Austen's time. Today it is an important nature reserve open to the public. The woodland is a mixture of oak, horse chestnut, sycamore and ash, with many informal footpaths. Crabtree is a hugely important site for butterflies. It attracts many different varieties due to its south facing position and the woodland and grassland is managed for flowering plants.

Crabtree Plantation, once part of the Hackwood Estate, is now an important nature reserve.

63

Overton

James Austen, Jane's eldest brother, became curate-in-charge of St Mary's church in March 1790.

FOR THE NEXT part of our journey we return to the Deane Gate Inn and this time head west along the B3400 towards Overton through the valley of the River Test, all the way to Whitchurch.

The self-sufficient little town of Overton with its eclectic mix of small businesses serves the wider community just as it did in Jane Austen's day. The road we are using was part of the main London to Exeter route which was 'turnpiked' in 1754 by an Act of Parliament. The toll-gate cottage where the pike (pole) barrier was operated is still there at the western boundary.

When James left here in 1796, William Harrison became rector of St Mary's and in 1817 was made vicar.

In those days Overton had two principal coaching inns standing at opposite corners of the cross roads with the route from Winchester to Newbury. The New Inn stood on the site now occupied by the Community Centre and Library. Here on 28 September 1810 a meeting was held with twenty prominent land and mill owners in attendance.

Lovelace Bigg-Wither was in the chair and others whom Jane knew well included Wither Bramston, John Harwood, William and John Portal, George Lefroy and the Rev. William Harrison. Their concern was a proposal to extend the Basingstoke Canal through their estates to join up with the Andover Canal.

The White Hart on the opposite corner from the Community Centre is still there but as I write, its future is uncertain. It is closed and up for sale. Jane and her family would have been very familiar with this inn. Throughout her lifetime a room in the hotel was used as a Magistrate's Court and this arrangement continued until 1895 when a new system of local government was established.

By the spring of 1790, Jane's brother James had finished his training to be a priest, and had become curate-in-charge at St Mary's church in Overton. He moved into the Old Rectory from where he indulged his passion for fox-hunting by riding out with the Kempshott pack. Whilst living in Overton he became acquainted with General Mathew of Laverstoke and started to court Anne, his daughter.

A couple of years later, George Austen appointed James as his curate at Deane in order to provide him with extra income to help support a wife. On 16 March 1792, in anticipation of the forthcoming nuptials, James ordered a houseful of new furniture and fittings from Ring's shop in Basingstoke, to be delivered to Deane Parsonage.

However, there was a problem. Mrs Lloyd and her two daughters Mary and Martha were still in residence and temporary arrangements had to be made. On 27 March James and Anne married at Laverstoke. They determined that the Overton Rectory was much too small for their needs and moved briefly into Court Farm House where they remained until June.

At Deane Parsonage in April 1793, Anne gave birth to a daughter who was christened Anna. Just two years later, Anne died suddenly leaving James alone to care for his baby daughter. After three years of widowerhood James turned his thoughts to taking a new wife. Abandoning hope of marrying his cousin, Eliza, he narrowed his choice to Mary Lloyd and Mary Harrison, who was another friend of the Austen sisters.

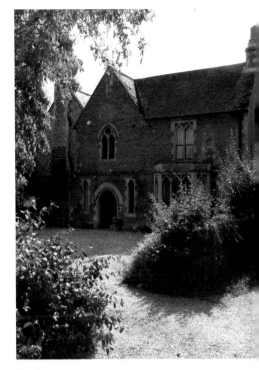

On his appointment as curate James moved into this small rectory near the church.

When James married Anne Mathew the couple moved briefly into the commodious Court Farm House next to the church.

This old painting shows the church and farmhouse as it would have appeared when James lived there.

In the event, James chose to marry Mary Lloyd. The couple were married on 17 January 1797 at Hurstbourne Tarrant and Mary moved back into the parsonage at Deane which she had been required to vacate five years earlier. Mary Harrison wasn't left long on the shelf. In September of that same year she married Philip Henry Poore a man midwife from Winchester and the couple moved to Andover. Jane maintained contact with Mary Harrison and she is mentioned in a couple of Jane's letters.

Mary's brother, the Reverend William Harrison, was by this time, vicar of Overton. William lived outside the parish (probably in Winchester) but needed to visit from time to time so, from 1810, took a lease on Rectory House.

In 1798, Overton boasted five grocers, a fishmonger, butcher, and a mercer selling textiles, a glazier and a clockmaker. You could buy suits, corsets, collars, breeches and shoes all made in the parish. We know that Jane used to shop in Overton from a letter she wrote to her sister, Cassandra on Sunday 25 November 1798, in which she said:

'The Overton Scotchman has been kind enough to rid me of some of my money, in exchange for six shifts and four pair of stockings. The Irish is not so fine as I should like

Below left: In this very early photograph of Winchester Street, the road is still unmade. John Irving's shop can be seen in the middle distance on the left.

Below right: A list of Overton tradesmen in 1798 shows the mercer John Irving, fifth from the bottom in the left-hand column.

286   OVERTON, HANTS.

Webb Thomas, Gent. (F.)
PHYSIC.
Brookman Robert, (F.) *Apothecary*
TRADERS, &c.
Alfin John, (F.)
Baker William, (F.) *Grocer*
Bartelotte John, *Victualler, (Greyhound)*
Beale Joseph, (F.) *Maltster*
Beazley John, *New Inn*
Blackburn John, (F.) *Carpenter*
Brown Robert, *Grocer*
Brown William, *Farmer*
Burges Thomas, *Brickmaker*
Chamberlin William, (F.) *Taylor*
Cook George, *Farmer*
Cooper Thomas, *Taylor*
Corps James, *Fellmonger*
Corps John, *Carpenter*
Craft John, *Breeches-maker*
Crimble James, (F.) *Miller*
Crockford James, *Grocer*
Cuffley Peter, (F.) *Blacksmith*
Dicker John, *Maltster*
Farley William, *Collar-maker*
Farmer Moses, (F.) *Farmer*
Flower Francis, (F.) *Farmer*
Gauntlet Gabriel, *Shoemaker*
Hammerton David, *Blacksmith*
Hankin William, *White Hart Inn*
Hunt John, *Clockmaker*
Hutchins George, *Butcher*
Husband George, *Staymaker*
Irving John, *Mercer*
Kercher Anthony, *Shoemaker*
Lamb George, (F.) *Oil and Colour Man*
Lambole George, *Hair-dresser*
Lyhood Gabriel, (F.)

Martin George, *Taylor*
Morrel Edmund, *Shoemaker*
Nash William, (F.) *Schoolmaster*
Nash William, *Parish-clerk*
Ofman James, *Warrener*
Paice William, (F.) *Victualler, (Red Lion)*
Pain Thomas, (F.) *Blacksmith*
Palmer Thomas, *Taylor*
Paskell William, (F.)
Penton Joseph, *Staymaker*
Pike Thomas, *Fishmonger*
Pink John, *Breeches-maker*
Pithouse Thomas, (F.) *Blacksmith*
Purdue Robert, *Bricklayer*
Purdue John, *Bricklayer*
Pyle William, *Grocer*
Pyle William, *Butcher*
Pyle Thomas, (F.) *Gardener*
Rawlins John, *Farmer*
Redsdall William, *Blacksmith*
Sawkins William, (F.) *Carpenter*
Small George, *Farmer*
Small Thomas, (F.) *Miller*
Small Thomas, *Maltster*
Smith Thomas, *Glazier*
Spier Edward, *Shoemaker*
Sprent William, *Schoolmaster*
Stephens John, *Shoemaker*
Thomas Elias, *Shoemaker*
Toogood William, *Grocer*
Toogood John, (F.)
Tyler Thomas, (F.) *Wheeler*
Venn Thomas, *Wheeler*
Ward John, *Farmer*
Webb John, *Miller*
Wiltshire Stephen, *Shoemaker*

The branch of HSBC bank that now occupies the site of Irving's shop.

The White Hart taken from the opposite corner of the crossroads where the New Inn formerly stood.

LONDON 54
BASINGSTOKE 8

The old toll cottage still stands at western boundary of Overton with the milestone set beside it for the benefit of stagecoaches.

it; but as I gave as much money for it as I intended, I have no reason to complain. It cost me 3s. 6d. per yard. It is rather finer, however, than our last, and not so harsh a cloth.'

'The Overton Scotchman' was John Irving, listed in a trade directory of that year as a mercer. The Austens would most likely have had a charge account with Mr Irving. Unfortunately, despite local protests, the shop was pulled down fairly recently and a branch of HSBC Bank now occupies the site. Prior to demolition it was still trading as a drapers.

On the approach to Overton from Deane the road dips steeply downhill and passes a spot which became very significant in Jane's life. This is where her great friend Mrs Anne Lefroy died in a riding accident on 16 December 1804.

Anne had ridden to Overton with a servant to do some shopping, and, meeting James Austen in the village, remarked prophetically on the stupidity and laziness of her horse. On the way home, something spooked the animal and it bolted. The servant couldn't catch it and, in trying to get off, Anne fell hitting her head on the hard road surface and died some hours later.

Jane was by now living in Bath. It was her twenty-ninth birthday and the loss affected her deeply. Four years later, on the anniversary of the tragic event, she wrote a long poem as a moving tribute to her friend.

In 1810 William Harrison took a lease on Rectory House.

Laverstoke & Freefolk Priors

THE B3400 CROSSES the River Test at Laverstoke 2 miles east of Whitchurch, where both road and river divide the hamlet of Freefolk Priors from the village of Laverstoke. This is the country of the Portals; a Huguenot family who were forced to leave France, as a result of religious persecution.

Henri de Portal settled in Hampshire in 1712 and bought a lease on Bere Mill in Whitchurch where he produced exceptionally hard and close-textured paper. Within

As I write, the Portal's old paper mill at Laverstoke is being converted into a new state-of-the-art distillery and visitors' centre, for the Bombay Sapphire gin brand owned by Bacardi

The old Freefolk Priors mansion with its Tudor origins was rented by General Mathew during Jane Austen's time.

twelve years he had taken English nationality and established a second paper mill at Laverstoke. Unprecedented success followed when in 1724, he acquired the exclusive right to produce the distinctive water-marked paper used for all bank notes issued by the Bank of England.

During the next generation of Portals the Austens had moved into the neighbourhood and the two families became friendly and socialized together. Jane would have been very familiar with Portal's industrial buildings in the otherwise rural landscape. For almost 300 years the Portals were the leading banknote paper manufacturer in the world.

In more recent times the business moved to neighbouring Overton and in 1995 was acquired by De la Rue. This enterprise, now lodged in a large factory at Overton railway station, produces the currency paper for virtually every country of the world, including the American dollar. They now also print banknotes and, ironically will soon be printing Jane's image on the next issue of the £10 note.

At the site of the historic Laverstoke Mill, construction work is underway to create a new state-of-the-art distillery and visitors' centre, for the Bombay Sapphire gin brand owned by Bacardi. The original buildings are being incorporated into the new development.

With the Portal family success, came wealth and property. In 1759 Joseph Portal, Henry's son, purchased the original Tudor manor house at Laverstoke which he later leased to fiery General Mathew, ex-Governor of Grenada. From 1763 Joseph also owned Ashe Park, which in 1793 was inherited by his son William who leased it for many years to James Holder.

James Austen married General Mathew's daughter Anne on 27 March 1792 in the little thirteenth-century church of St Nicholas at Freefolk. Revd George Austen took the service. The seventeen-year-old Jane may well have been present at the ceremony because the church was within easy reach of her home at Steventon.

St Nicholas, with its pretty bell turret, is now a redundant church under the care of the Churches Conservation Trust. It has many treasures including an early fifteenth-century wall-painting of St Christopher and a colourful and intricately carved Jacobean monument to Sir Richard Powlett, who died in 1614.

The Portals had extensive social contacts with the Austens and later connections through marriage. In the first available letter we have from Jane, written at Steventon on 9 January 1796 when she was twenty-one, she mentions members of the Portal family being present at the Basingstoke Assembly balls:

'We had an exceeding good ball last night ... we had the Grants, St Johns, Lady Rivers, her three daughters and a son, Mr. and Miss Heathcote, Mrs Lefevre, two Mr. Watkins, Mr J. Portal, Miss Deanes, two Miss Ledgers, and a tall clergyman who came with them. ...' She goes on to inform Cassandra: 'We had a visit yesterday morning from Mr. Benjamin Portal, whose eyes are as handsome as ever.'

The present-day Laverstoke House was built in 1798 for Harry Portal on an elevated site on the other side of the river and the old house was demolished. The construction of the new house provided Jane with the name Joseph Bonomi, the architect mentioned in *Sense & Sensibility* who was responsible for the country house plans that the insufferable Robert Ferrars flung onto the fire.

'For my own part,' said he, 'I am excessively fond of a cottage; there is always so much comfort, so much elegance about them. And I protest, if I had any money to spare, I should buy a little land and build one myself, within a short distance of London, where I might drive myself down at any time, and collect a few friends about me, and be happy. I advise everybody who is going to build, to build a cottage. My friend Lord Courtland came to me the other day on purpose to ask my advice, and laid before me three different

Jane may well have been present in St Nicholas's church at Freefolk Priors on 27 March 1792 when her brother James Austen married Anne Mathew with Revd George Austen officiating.

Laverstoke House is now home to former Formula One World Champion racing driver Jody Scheckter.

plans of Bonomi's. I was to decide on the best of them. "My dear Courtland," said I, immediately throwing them all into the fire, "do not adopt either of them, but by all means build a cottage." And that I fancy, will be the end of it.'

As Bonomi's neoclassical house was a novelty in North Hampshire it was much discussed locally and his name became more or less a household word. The house was later owned by the Sheffield family and sold in 1996 to its present owner Jody Scheckter, the former South African Formula One World Champion, who after retiring took up commercial organic farming at Laverstoke Park Farm.

Bank note paper continues to be manufactured at nearby Overton with the £10 note featuring a tribute to the genius of a local Hampshire girl.

Whitchurch

JANE HAD TO pass through Whitchurch on her visits to and from the Lloyds' home at Ibthorpe. In her letter to Cassandra of 30 November 1800 she says: 'Martha has promised to return with me & our plan is to [have] a nice black frost for walking to Whitchurch & there throw ourselves into a postchaise one upon the other, our heads hanging out at one door, and our feet at the opposite'.

From the Lloyd's house at Ibthorpe it is an 8 mile walk to Whitchurch, so it is easy to see the girls throwing themselves into the carriage with a certain amount of relief and abandonment. A postchaise was a closed two-horse carriage used to transport post and passengers with the post-boy riding one of the horses; it was the nearest equivalent the Georgians had to a taxi.

The imposing red-brick Town Hall was built during the reign of Queen Anne.

This impressive white painted inn was well known to Jane. It stands at the junction of the old London to Exeter and Oxford to Southampton roads.

The postchaise could have been hired from the White Hart which stands at the junction of the old London to Exeter and Oxford to Southampton roads. The impressive white-painted inn can trace its origins to 1461. The present building, dates from around 1700, and is transitional between the Stuart and Queen Anne Styles of architecture. Another of the Whitchurch buildings Jane would have known is the imposing red-brick Town Hall, built during the reign of Queen Anne; it stands directly facing the junction with the road to Steventon.

As previously mentioned Huguenot refugee, Henri de Portal, settled in Hampshire in 1712 and purchased the lease on Bere Mill on the eastern side of Whitchurch. From here he produced exceptionally hard and close-textured paper. In 1815, Henry Hayter built a second mill at Whitchurch which, a couple of years later, was acquired by William Maddick, a silk manufacturer from Spitalfields.

In 1712, Henri de Portal, a Huguenot refugee from France took a lease on Bere Mill
and started the paper-making tradition that continues today at Overton.

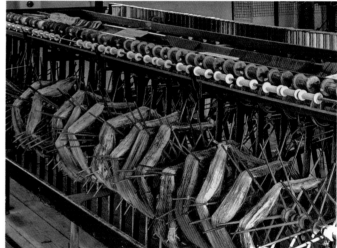

Left: Jane was living in Chawton when the Whitchurch Silk Mill was built in 1815 by Henry Hayter.
Top: The process of silk taffeta being woven on a nineteenth-century tappet loom can still be seen today at Whitchurch Silk Mill.
Above: Colourful silks ready for winding on to bobbins at the Whitchurch mill.

Visiting mills was a tourist pastime in Jane's day as we learn from a letter written by her friend Mrs Anne Lefroy on 17 June 1801. Her party visited Portal's paper mill but the silk mill she refers to was at Overton and is no longer operational: 'The two Miss Carletons Miss [Vyse] & Miss Speed came to spend the day in the morning we went first to the Silk & then to the Paper Mills.'

At the time of Anne Lefroy's visit, Streatwells mill at Overton and Maddick's mill at Whitchurch were the largest employers in the area. The workforce was mainly women, sometimes up to eighty years of age, and children from the age of six. It was not until the year following Anne Lefroy's visit that the Factory Act came into force, limiting the work of children in textile mills to twelve hours a day. This was largely ignored by employers.

When Henri Portal moved his operations on to Laverstoke and Quidhampton, Bere Mill changed to flour milling. It can still be seen today. The Silk Mill at Whitchurch is now a popular visitor attraction. Many of the 1990 television adaptations of Jane Austen's novels used the Whitchurch mill to provide fabric for costumes and they have a small display showing stills from various productions including, the film biography 'Becoming Jane'.

Like New York cabs, a postchaise was always painted yellow and was sometimes referred to as 'a yellow bounder'. It was controlled by a postilion riding one of the horses.

Hurstbourne Tarrant & Ibthorpe

WILLIAM COBBETT, FAMOUS pamphleteer, farmer and fearless journalist was a contemporary of Jane Austen and a regular visitor to Rookery Farmhouse across the road from the White Hart at Hurstbourne Tarrant. This area is known as the Hampshire Highlands and Cobbett has given us this description:

Above the gently curving meadows beyond the village, rise the steep-wooded hillsides famously known as the 'hangers' of Hampshire.

'This, to my fancy, is a very nice country. It is continual hill and dell. Now and then a chain of hills higher than the rest, and these are downs or woods. This place is commonly called Uphusband, as decent a corruption of names as one would wish to meet with. However, Uphusband the people will have it. The houses of the village are in great part, scattered about, and are amongst very lofty and fine trees, the village is a sight beyond description.'

Jane was also very well acquainted with Uphusband, known today as Hurstbourne Tarrant, through her visits to Ibthorpe, the smaller hamlet to the north west, which she

Opposite: Ibthorpe House, near Hurstbourne Tarrant was the home of Martha and Mary Lloyd with whom Jane often stayed.

always called Ibthrop. In the summer of 1792 Jane's great friend Martha Lloyd moved to Ibthorpe House with her spinster sister Mary and their widowed mother. Jane and Cassandra stayed with them during October of the same year.

The Lloyds had been tenants of the Austens, taking over Deane Parsonage in 1789 but vacating it three years later to make it available for James Austen and his first wife, Anne Mathew. At the time of Jane's first visit to Ibthorpe, two months before her seventeenth birthday, she attended her first formal dance. It was held at Knights Enham near Andover, home to David and Elizabeth Dewar. Elizabeth Dewar was Anne Mathew's sister. She had married David Dewar, the son of a wealthy West Indian planter of Scottish descent who had inherited the estate of Knights Enham from his father.

There is nothing to see today that Jane would have known. The house was destroyed by fire in 1883 and a new mansion was built. From 1918 it was developed as a centre for the rehabilitation of disabled service men returning from the First World War. In 1945 a substantial donation of £225,000 was made by the people of Egypt in gratitude for help they received during the battle of El Alamein in the Second World War. In 1995 Enham became a residential care home and is now known as Enham Alamein.

Jane and Cassandra were accompanied to the Enham dance by Mary and Martha Lloyd. Before returning to Steventon, the Austen ladies also attended a ball at Hurstbourne Park just west of Whitchurch. This was the home of John Charles Wallop, Lord Lymington, 3rd Earl of Portsmouth. It might seem like a daunting prospect for the seventeen-year-old daughter of a country parson to visit such a grand house but John Charles had been a friend from her childhood. He had maintained a friendship with the Austen family from the time he had been a pupil of George Austen's at Steventon.

Mrs Austen had commented, when John Charles lived with them, on the backwardness of the little boy and as he grew up, his mental condition worsened. However, in spite of his handicap, he was married off in 1814 to Mary-Anne-Hanson, daughter of the family lawyer. It was a bad move.

Mary-Anne cuckolded the Earl by entering into a very public adulterous relationship. She locked up her mad husband and treated him with great cruelty whipping him on a regular basis. It wasn't long before Mary-Anne brought her lover William Rowland Alder into the house and they went on to have three children together. The Earl was formally declared insane many years after Jane's death and Mary-Anne was then able to marry her adulterous lover.

James Austen was widowed after only three years of marriage to Anne Mathew and, in what seems a rather curious turn of events, he chose Mary Lloyd as his second wife. The couple were married here in Hurstbourne Tarrant on 17 January 1797 in the church of St Peter. Mary consequently moved back into the parsonage at Deane that she had vacated five years earlier to make room for James and his first wife.

On 19 November 1800 we hear from Jane of another ball at Hurstbourne Park which Charles Austen travelled from Gosport on the south coast especially to attend. He and Jane walked from Steventon to dine at Deane and then went on with James and Mary to Lord Portsmouth's estate where Jane had a very good time:

'I believe I drank too much wine last night at Hurstbourne; I know not how else to account for the shaking of my hand today ... There were only twelve dances, of which I danced nine, & was merely prevented from dancing the rest by the want of a partner ...There were very few Beauties, and such as there were, were not very handsome. Miss Iremonger did not look well, & Mrs Blount was the only one much admired. She appeared exactly as she did in September, with the same broad face, diamond bandeau, white shoes, pink husband, & fat neck.'

Whilst staying at Ibthorpe Jane would have been very aware of the Blount's house at Rookery Farm, near the crossroads at the foot of Hurstbourne Hill. In addition to Mrs Blount, some other guests who come under Jane's scrutiny at the Hurstbourne Park ball

The George and Dragon coaching inn stands at the cross-roads in the centre of the village.

The Blount's house at Rookery Farm, is near the crossroads at the foot of Hurstbourne Hill.

83

were the Debary sisters. The Reverend Peter Debary, vicar of Hurstbourne, had four daughters, Ann, Sarah, Susannah and Mary: 'Miss Debary, Susan & Sally ... made their appearance, & I was as civil to them as their bad breath would allow me.'

Peter Debary and Joseph Blount were both wardens of a charity called Bunnys Gift. Mary Lloyd remained friends with the Debarys after she had left Ibthorpe. In November 1799 Miss Debary travelled to Deane to supervise the household when Mary was having her first child.

In a letter dated Friday 28 November 1800, written at Ibthorpe, we learn from Jane that she had: 'the pleasure of spending my time very pleasantly' despite wet weather which made it 'too dirty even for such desperate walkers as Martha and I to get out of doors'. In this letter there is further mention of the Debarys who lived in the parsonage next door to the church. The church of St Peter is about a mile from Ibthorpe House and Jane and the Lloyds would have worshipped there.

'Three of the Miss Debaries called here the morning after my arrival, but I have not yet been able to return their civility;- You know it is not an uncommon circumstance in this parish to have the road from Ibthrop to the Parsonage much dirtier & more impracticable

Right from the beginning of her dancing days Jane's letters are full of descriptions of the people she observes at the balls.

Jane made visits to the parsonage home of the Debarys which stands next to the church.

SACRED TO THE MEMORY OF
SARAH,
YOUNGEST DAUGHTER OF THE LATE REV.ᵈ PETER DEBARY
AND ANN HIS WIFE,
WHO DEPARTED THIS LIFE THE 7ᵀᴴ OF JANUARY 1828,
THE PLACE OF HER INTERMENT IS
NEAR THE TOMB OF HER PARENTS.
ALSO OF ANN HER ELDEST SISTER
WHO DIED SEPTEMBER XI 1851

ALSO OF SUSANNAH THEIR SISTER, WHO DIED
THE 15ᵀ NOVEMBER 1852, AGED 84.
ALSO OF MARY THEIR SISTER, WHO DIED
THE 8ᵀᴴ OCTOBER 1854, AGED 89.

The memorial to the 'endless'
Debary sisters in St Peter's.

St Peter's church where James
Austen married Mary Lloyd on
17 January 1797.

Knights Enham Rectory, home to the Atkinson sisters who attended the ball: *'fat girls with small noses'*.

for walking than the road from the Parsonage to Ibthrop… The Endless Debaries are of course very well acqainted with the lady who is to marry Sir Thomas, & all her family. I pardon them however, as their description of her is favourable...'

There is a monument to the Debary girls in St Peter's church which depicts a standing woman by a sarcophagus. Jane returned to Steventon in the December to be greeted with the news that her family was moving to Bath, and family tradition has it that she 'fainted away', because the shock was so great.

Cassandra helped Martha nurse Mrs Lloyd in her final illness. After Mrs Lloyd died at Ibthorpe in April 1805, Martha moved in with the Austens at Bath, and stayed with them after the move to Chawton in 1809. It was a happy arrangement and lasted about twenty years altogether. She eventually became Francis Austen's second wife in 1828, when she was aged sixty-two.

Reverend Atkinson's church of St Michael and All Angels at Enham.

The modern mansion at Hurstbourne can only be glimpsed from a distance.

Andover

JAMES AUSTEN WAS widowed in 1795 and was left to care for his baby daughter Anna. When the appropriate time came for him to think of re-marrying, according to family tradition, he first had an infatuation with his glamorous cousin Eliza de Feuillide. When things didn't work out in that direction he turned his attention to two local Marys: Martha Lloyd's sister Mary and Mary Harrison whose brother William became vicar of Overton at the time James left the parish for Deane.

In one of her early letters to Cassandra, Jane asks this question: 'Let me know how J. Harwood deports himself without the Miss Biggs – and which of the Marys will carry the day with my Brother James.'

This fine Georgian building which Jane visited is now home to the Andover Museum.

James ultimately favoured Mary Lloyd but Jane kept contact with Mary Harrison who subsequently married Philip-Henry Poore, a surgeon apothecary and man-midwife from Andover. Mary moved in to Philip's elegant town house at 6 Church Close which is now home to the town museum.

Before she married Philip, Mary is mentioned in a couple of Jane's letters. The first dated 5 September 1796 was written from Rowling in Kent and has this intriguing comment: 'Give my love to Mary Harrison & tell her I wish whenever she is attached to a young Man, some respectable Dr Marchmont may keep them apart for five volumes.'

This is a reference to the novel *Marchmont* by Charlotte Turner Smith, the English Romantic poet and novelist. Charlotte helped establish the conventions of Gothic fiction, and also wrote political novels of sensibility. Although Jane is mocking Charlotte, some academics have suggested her own style owes something to Smith's novels.

The 'extolled' staircase
at 6 Church Close.

A Georgian tableau in the
museum which was formerly the
home of Philip and Mary Poore.

A couple of years after writing this letter, Jane began working on *Northanger Abbey* (initially titled *Susan*), her parody of the Gothic genre.

In the following extract from a letter to Cassandra dated 30 November 1800 Jane revealed that she called at 6 Church Close and 'mounted the highly-extolled Staircase'.

'I spent an hour in Andover, of which Messre Painter and Redding has the larger part – twenty minutes however fell to the lot of Mrs Poore and her mother, whom I was glad to see in good looks and spirits. – The latter asked me more questions than I had very well time to answer; I mounted the highly-extolled Staircase & went into the elegant Drawing -Room, which I fancy is now Mrs Harrison's apartment;- and in short did everything that extraordinary Abilities can be supposed to compass in so short a time.'

As you might guess, 'Messre Painter and Redding' were shopkeepers. Thomas Painter was a haberdasher and Grace Redding was a linen and woollen draper. From Jane's tone, it seems that other people must also have mentioned how grand the Poore's staircase was. It is located on the left hand side of the building, set in its own staircase hall leading off from the main entrance to the museum.

The fact that Jane was under time pressure, suggests she might have been changing coaches here, connecting with one to take her to Ibthorpe. In Jane's time Andover was a transportation hub where the busy London to Exeter and the Southampton to Oxford routes crossed. Thirty coaches a day passed through the town which had developed into a major coaching stage.

A couple of the old coaching inns the Austens would have known remain, although greatly reduced in size. The stable yards of others have been transformed into shopping arcades and are remembered now only by the names.

The Angel in Upper High Street is Andover's oldest surviving inn. The original twelfth-century building was destroyed in the great fire of Andover in 1435 and was re-built ten years later by the owners, Winchester College. This was a galleried inn and traces of the old gallery can still be seen although it is now enclosed.

The Angel, in Upper High Street is Andover's oldest surviving inn.

The much reduced George Inn where William Cobbett caused a near riot in 1826 with his speech on the Corn Laws.

Above right: A pavement mosaic in front of the George denotes the importance of Andover as a major coaching town.

For centuries the Angel Inn had been the resort of royalty and the rich and famous. Catherine of Aragon, the first wife of Henry VIII, stayed here in 1501 on her way from Plymouth to London. George III stayed here on several occasions during Jane's lifetime on his frequent journeys to and from his favourite seaside resort of Weymouth. At that time the inn boasted spacious gardens at the back and even had its own farm which stood on the corner of Winchester Street and Old Winton Road and ran all along the back of Love Lane.

In the 1820s the front bar of the inn served temporarily as Guildhall and Magistrates' Court while the construction of the present building was taking place. The classical Georgian Guildhall commanding the High Street is a re-build of the one Jane knew.

The town you see today has undergone a dramatic change since the Georgian era. This was particularly so from 1961 when it was greatly expanded with large housing and industrial estates as part of the policy of dispersal from London. Luckily there are still corners of antiquity to be discovered for those who seek them.

The classical Georgian Guildhall commanding the High Street is a re-build of the one Jane knew.

Jane would have known these sixteenth-century half-timbered houses in Chantry Street which runs down from the church.

91

Southampton

JANE'S FIRST EXPERIENCE of Southampton was very nearly her last. In the late summer of 1783, when she was seven and Cassandra was ten, they were receiving private tuition in the city when a typhus outbreak occurred. By the time Mrs Austen received the news both her daughters were infected. They eventually recovered but their aunt, Mrs Cooper, did not. When she collected her own daughter from Southampton she caught the fever and died a few days after reaching her home.

Luckily Jane and Cassandra's next visit to the town, a decade later, was a much happier event. It was the winter of 1793 and their brother Francis had returned home after five years' service in the Far East. He was able to escort his sisters from Steventon to Southampton to visit their relations, the Butler-Harrisons. Elizabeth Matilda Austen, a cousin from Kent, had married John Butler-Harrison who was an important figure in the town. He had been sheriff in 1790 then mayor in 1794 and again in 1811.

Some years later, Jane remembered celebrating her eighteenth birthday, during that 1793 holiday, when she and Cassandra danced happily at the Dolphin Inn in the beautiful bow-windowed room on the first floor which can still be visited today. According to her letters, Jane attended two other dances in the town's Assembly Rooms.

Jane's third visit to Southampton was longer term. This time she became resident from the autumn of 1806 until the spring of 1809, a period of two and a half years. The family had been living in Bath from the time of Revd Austen's retirement in 1801. Following his death in 1805, Mrs Austen considered settling temporarily with her newly married son Frank, who was renting lodgings in Southampton.

Frank was by now a naval captain with a pleasant young wife, Mary Gibson. By the time Mrs Austen had made the decision and the move, it was early in 1807. The Austen ladies were accompanied by Martha Lloyd, who had lived with them since her mother's death nearly two years earlier. By the time the full party finally arrived at Southampton, Frank and Mary's first child was on the way.

Jane's brother Frank spent most of his long life on active duty in the Royal Navy. He became Sir Francis William Austen, GCB rising to the position of Admiral of the Fleet.

The Austens' house stood a little way inland from this section of the medieval walls which in those days were lapped by the sea.

Number 3 Castle Square stood somewhere near the present day Juniper Berry public house. It had delightful views over Southampton Water to the New Forest and steps from the garden gave access to the ramparts.

Frank's original lodgings were expensive and they soon all moved into a 'commodious old-fashioned' house in Castle Square, which was rented from the second Marquess of Lansdowne. The house was in a pleasant if rather curious situation. Just two years before the Austens arrived, the Marquess had built a Gothic fantasy castle in the middle of the square on the ruins of the central keep of the original medieval castle.

Jane refers to this as 'the fantastic edifice'. She and her family enjoyed watching the equally eccentric Marchioness drive out in 'a light phaeton drawn by six or eight ponies in graduated shades of brown'. The Austens' address was 3 Castle Square, but the precise location of the house is not known. The most likely spot is near the present-day Juniper Berry public house in modern Upper Bugle Street.

Although Jane never liked living in a town, there was some compensation in the fact that the old house had a large garden. She began a plan to plant it with flowering shrubs and fruit trees and mentions currants and gooseberry bushes as well as raspberries and tells

Two years before the Austens moved in, their landlord, the Marquess of Lansdowne built a Gothic fantasy castle in the middle of the square which Jane refers to as 'the fantastic edifice'.

us 'We hear that we are envied our house by many people and that the garden is the best in town.'

Steps up from the end of the garden provided the family with access to the promenade along the top of the walls. From here there was a delightful view westwards across Southampton Water to the New Forest. Today, however, this section of the walls looks down on reclaimed land which is used for industrial purposes.

The town Jane knew was more a sea-bathing spa than a port. John Gilpin, has provided us with a description: 'It is an elegant well built town. It stands on the confluence of 2 large waters and when the tide is full is seated on a peninsula. It is a town of great antiquity and still preserves its respectable appendages of ancient walls and gates. The country around is beautiful.'

Summer balls were held in the Long Rooms which stood near Westgate. In the winter, assembly balls were held once a fortnight in the Dolphin Inn. Jane took out a subscription to these, and before leaving Southampton she decided to take full advantage of her social

The High Street pictured in 1808, when the town was less a port and more a spa. There are many references to Jane and family members walking here during summer evenings. The classical building on the left is All Saints' church where the Austen family worshipped.

Jane took out a subscription to the balls held here at the Dolphin Hotel.

The Dolphin ballroom where Jane danced can still be visited today.

opportunities: 'A larger circle of acquaintance and an increase of amusement is quite in character with our approaching removal. Yes, I mean to go to as many balls as possible that I may have a good bargain.' Following a ball at the Dolphin on 9 December 1808, Jane wrote to Cassandra:

'Our ball was rather more amusing than I expected… The room was tolerably full, and there were, perhaps, thirty couple of dancers… It was the same room in which we danced fifteen years ago. I thought it all over, and in spite of the shame of being so much older, felt with thankfulness that I was quite as happy now as then. We paid an additional shilling for our tea, which we took as we chose in an adjoining and very comfortable room… You will not expect to hear that I was asked to dance, but I was…'

As well as the Assembly Rooms there were fine shops, circulating libraries, a theatre and opportunities for river trips and visits to the romantic ruined abbeys at Beaulieu and Netley.

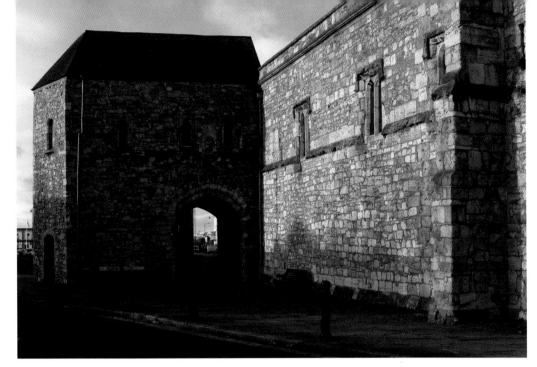

God's House Gate which Jane would have passed through in order to access the beach and Town Quay. In the eighteenth-century the tower was used as a debtors' prison and felons' gaol.

The Cross House ferry shelter where Jane would have waited for the ferryman prior to her trips on the river.

Jane would pass this magnificent house on her way to the Assembly Rooms. The Tudor House and Garden are open to the public and reveal over eight-hundred years of history in the heart of the Old Town.

Summer balls were held in the Long Rooms which stood near here at Westgate. In 1620 the sailors and passengers of the *Mayflower* passed through this gate on their way to America.

Southampton Environs

IN ADDITION TO the Austen's large garden at 3 Castle Square, Southampton's proximity to the water made amends for Jane having to live in a town. She delighted in long walks through the surrounding countryside and enjoyed boat trips when relatives visited.

Edward Austen-Knight and his wife Elizabeth brought three of their children to Hampshire in the summer of 1807. The diary of their eldest daughter Fanny records several water excursions. The entry for Monday 14 September tells of Fanny shopping at the market with G'mama and taking a long walk to the ferry before breakfast. From the following day's entry we get a clue to the impending tragedy which was soon to befall Edward's family, when Fanny tells us:

'We went in a hired boat to Hythe to call on Mrs Palmer who called on us the day before. Mama to every body's astonishment was of the party, & not at all sick. In the evening uncle Henry A. came. Aunt C. & I walked in the High Street till late.'

A popular excursion was to Netley Abbey, a picturesque ruin 4 miles across the water from Southampton. A party was made up and Fanny noted in her diary for Wednesday 16 September: 'We all except Grandmama took a boat & went to Netley Abbey the ruins of which look beautiful. We eat there of some biscuits we had taken, & returned quite delighted. Aunt Jane and I walked in the High Street till late.'

In a subsequent letter to her former governess, Miss Chapman, Fanny gave a full description of 'the beautiful ruins' and the effect which they had on her: '...never was there anything in the known world to be compared to that compound of everything that is striking, ancient, & Majestic, we were struck dumb with admiration.'

Other visitors to the ruins objected to the stalls selling toys and gingerbread, and the presence of picnickers popping ginger beer. At the time of the Austen's visit to the abbey it stood in a wooded area that stretched down to the water's edge. Founded in 1239, the abbey is still substantial and quietly impressive. Today it is surrounded on all sides by modern housing but it is still well worth a visit.

A popular excursion was to Netley Abbey, a picturesque ruin 4 miles across the water from Southampton.

Founded in 1239, Netley Abbey is still substantial and quietly impressive. Traces of the red Tudor bricks of Sir William Paulet's mansion can still be seen.

Various claims (including some at the site itself) that Jane was influenced by seeing the ruins when writing *Northanger Abbey* are not founded. Her novel was written a decade before the Austen family's excursion to Netley.

Following the dissolution of Netley Abbey on 3 August 1536, King Henry VIII granted the abbey buildings to Sir William Paulet, his Lord Treasurer. As soon as he took over, Sir William started the process of turning the abbey into a palace and traces of the red Tudor bricks he used in converting the buildings into a series of luxurious apartments can still be seen. Later, changing attitudes led to the Tudor alterations being removed and the abbey ruins were returned to their romantic elegance.

On Thursday 17 September 1807 Fanny gives us an account of another outing. This time Uncle Henry hired a 'sociable' and took members of the family for a drive in the New Forest visiting Lyndhurst and Lymington. A sociable (short for sociable coach) is an open, four-wheeled carriage having two double seats facing each other. Fanny records: 'We took some cold partridges, enjoyed ourselves very much, & returned at ½ past 5 to dinner.'

Three weeks later the family at Castle Square received the news that Elizabeth had died suddenly following the birth of her eleventh child. The two eldest boys, George and Edward junior were at school in Winchester. Jane expressed a desire to help, so they came to stay with her at Southampton.

Jane did her best to comfort and amuse the boys. She played games like spillikins and cards, told them riddles and jokes, and encouraged them to make paper boats and sink them with horse chestnuts. Reporting to Cassandra in a letter written at the house in Castle Square on Monday 24 October Jane says:

'We had a little water party yesterday; I and my two nephews went from the Itchen Ferry up to Northam, where we landed, looked into the 74, and walked home, and it was so much enjoyed that I had intended to take them to Netley to-day; the tide is just right for

One can imagine the Austens picnicking on their cold partridges in the ruins of Netley Abbey or a quiet New Forest glade.

On Thursday 17 September 1807 Uncle Henry hired a 'sociable' and took the family for a drive in the New Forest where wild ponies have grazed for thousands of years.

our going immediately after noonshine, but I am afraid there will be rain; if we cannot get so far, however, we may perhaps go round from the ferry to the quay.'

'I had not proposed doing more than cross the Itchen yesterday, but it proved so pleasant, and so much to the satisfaction of all, that when we reached the middle of the stream we agreed to be rowed up the river; both the boys rowed a great part of the way, and their questions and remarks, as well as their enjoyment, were very amusing; George's enquiries were endless, and his eagerness in everything reminds me often of his Uncle Henry.'

Bucklers Hard is now preserved as a maritime museum with some of the shipwrights' cottages open to view.

The shoreline would have been buzzing with activity around half-built ships.

The 74 they looked into was HMS *Victorious*, a 74-gun third-rate ship of the line of the Royal Navy, built by Henry Adams and launched at nearby Bucklers Hard four days earlier. *Victorious's* first action came the following year when she assisted in the bombardment of the port of Flushing. She later served as part of Rear Admiral Sir George Cockburn's fleet in Chesapeake Bay during the American War of 1812.

In Jane's day Bucklers Hard was a working shipyard with five launch-ways. Fifty Royal Navy vessels were built at Bucklers Hard during Jane's lifetime, including three of the ships for Nelson's Trafalgar fleet. The shoreline would have been buzzing with activity around half-built ships, smoke billowing from smithies, ox-carts plodding up the main thoroughfare and barges jostling for space to unload supplies at the wharf.

Jane's Southampton sojourn was short lived. The newly widowed Edward decided it would be better if the family were a little closer together, so he offered his mother and sisters a choice of a house near Godmersham in Kent or one at Chawton. As we know, the Austens decided on the latter. The ladies left Southampton in April and, after a couple of visits to relatives, moved to Chawton in July 1809.

The present day busy little ferry that plies between Hythe and Hamble-le-Rice.

Portsmouth

ON FRIDAY 15 July 1791 Jane's youngest brother, twelve-year-old Charles, entered the Royal Navy Academy at Portsmouth. The family made the trip for this occasion and it seems likely that sixteen-year-old Jane would have been included in the party. Jane's other sailor brother Frank, who was a year older than herself, had entered the Academy five years earlier and graduated in 1788.

In 1801 Frank was appointed Captain of HMS *Neptune* but a year later the temporary Peace of Amiens meant that he and his men were paid off at Portsmouth. His parents, together with his brother James and wife Mary, visited the town and boarded the *Neptune* to see the conditions below decks of a man-of-war. Jane was not present this time as she and Cassandra were at Godmersham.

In fact, there is no record of Jane visiting the town, but the accuracy of her Portsmouth descriptions in *Mansfield Park* confirms that she must have known it in some detail. She reveals an understanding of the geography, the dockyard area and the back streets with their slovenly womenfolk and rowdy children. During the years 1807 to 1809, when she was living in Southampton with Frank's family, it is assumed that he escorted her on trips to Portsmouth.

In those days, a single woman walking abroad in a naval port and garrison town like Portsmouth would have required a male escort. The High Street had some handsome Georgian houses and shops catering to the affluent residents but venturing off the main thoroughfare, Jane would have found filthy streets, appalling slums and abject poverty. The town had no water mains until 1811, and no drainage except the gutters which ran into the moat where everything including sewage was emptied.

If we take Fanny Price's opinion to be that of her creator, Jane did not seem to appreciate the people of Portsmouth. 'The men appeared to her all coarse, the women all pert, every body under-bred.' George Pinchard, a contemporary of Jane's, writing in 1795, was more direct: 'In some places Portsmouth is not only filthy but crowded with a class of low and abandoned beings. The riotous, drunken and immoral scenes of the place exceed all others.'

Standing on Old Portsmouth's Camber Dock, The Bridge Tavern has a huge flank wall mural based on Thomas Rowlandson's cartoon 'Portsmouth Point' which graphically shows how rough this area was in Jane's time.

Jane would have passed through this gateway to gain entrance to the town. It is now a gate to a naval sports field.

In *Mansfield Park*, Fanny Price is escorted by her brother William on a journey to revisit her parents after an absence of a dozen years. On the second day of the journey from Northamptonshire they arrived: '...in the environs of Portsmouth while there was yet daylight for Fanny to look around her, and wonder at the new buildings.'

Fanny and William would have passed through the Landport Gate into the town: '...the light was only beginning to fail as, guided by William's powerful voice, they were rattled into a narrow street, leading from the High Street, and drawn up before the door of a small house now inhabited by Mr. Price.' Second World War bombing has left little of the

105

Perhaps Lombard Street was the narrow street Jane had in mind for the location of the Prices' house.

Portsmouth Jane knew, but perhaps the narrow street she had in mind could have been Peacock Lane or Lombard Street where some seventeenth century houses survive.

Fanny Price left Portsmouth to live with her aunt and her family at Mansfield Park when she was ten years old, leaving behind a household in poor financial straits, a disorganised mother, and a father who: '...did not want abilities, but had no curiosity, and no information beyond his profession; he read only the newspaper and the navy-list; he talked only of the dock-yard, the harbour, Spithead, and the Motherbank.'

Fanny entered the house through a mean corridor off which opened a parlour: 'so small that her first conviction was of its being only a passage-room to something better…Fanny was almost stunned. The smallness of the house and thinness of the walls brought everything so close to her, that, added to the fatigue of her journey, and all her recent agitation, she hardly knew how to bear it.'

Unhappily established in her old home, Fanny is surprised and dismayed when Mr Crawford arrives. Not one to take no for an answer, he had come to Portsmouth to press his proposal to Fanny. He continues to stalk her and turns up the following Sunday: 'The Prices were just setting off for church … when Mr Crawford appeared again … he was asked to go with them to the Garrison Chapel, which was exactly what he had intended.'

The Royal Garrison Church was constructed about 1212. Then called the Domus Dei, it was part of a hospital complex for the old and the sick. Although the nave was badly damaged in a 1941 fire-bomb raid on Portsmouth, the chancel has been restored as a beautiful memorial to the men of the garrison who lost their lives in the Second World War but the nave remains a roofless ruin.

'In chapel they were obliged to divide, but Mr. Crawford took care not to be divided from the female branch; and after chapel he still continued with them, and made one in the family party on the ramparts.'

In Jane's time the ramparts completely surrounded the town on the land side. A short stretch overlooking the sea survives. It is here that Mr Crawford and the Price family would have climbed the steps to commence their walk: 'It was her [Mrs Price's] public place; there she met her acquaintance, heard a little news, talked over the badness of the Portsmouth servants, and wound up her spirits for the six days ensuing.'

The ramparts and saluting platform referred to by Mr Price.

The ramparts where Fanny Price walked during her visit to her parents.

The town has strong connections with Admiral Lord Nelson, whose flagship HMS *Victory* sailed from Portsmouth for the Battle of Trafalgar in 1805.

Mr Price tells Crawford: 'I was upon the platform two hours this afternoon, looking at her [the Thrush]. She lays close to the *Endymion*, between her and the *Cleopatra*, just to the eastward of the sheer hulk.' The platform Mr Price refers to was the Saluting Platform, adjacent to the northern end of the surviving ramparts. The 'sheer hulk' was a maintenance and repair vessel used to replace masts and spars. The *Endymion*, a sixth-rater with 24 guns and the *Cleopatra*, a fifth-rater with 38 guns, were both ships on which Charles Austen had served.

The Saluting Platform was built in the 1490s to welcome foreign ships and visiting royalty. On one occasion, Queen Elizabeth I visited the town and was not greeted by the firing of guns. When she complained, the Military Governor explained the Saluting Platform was in such a sorry state they dare not fire the guns. The Queen organized a raffle in the City of London to finance the Platform's repair.

The Royal Navy Academy that
Francis and Charles Austen
attended.

The entrance to Portsmouth
harbour seen from the end
of the ramparts.

The naval dockyard, founded by Henry VII towards the end of the fifteenth-century. It is now home to HMS *Victory*.

HMS *Victory* gun deck. The Austen family would have witnessed a similar scene when they visited HMS *Neptune* in 1801 when it was captained by Frank.

Watercolour of the beach at Portsmouth c.1808 with naval ships in the background.

'The conclusion of the two gentlemen's civilities was an offer of Mr Price's to take Mr Crawford into the dockyard.' Little is actually said about the dockyard itself aside from the party finding a seat on a vessel in the stocks. It seems odd to clamber on board a ship under construction just to sit down but at least we know from the remark they must have followed the same route as today's visitors take to view Nelson's flagship, HMS *Victory*, and Henry VIII's warship, the *Mary Rose*.

The Royal Naval Academy, in which both Francis and Charles Austen trained to become naval officers, was in the dockyard. The handsome red brick building remains but naval training there ceased in 1837.

In February 1801 the HMS *Endymion* made port at Portsmouth and the considerate Lieutenant Charles Austen arrived bearing gifts for his two sisters; the famous topaz crosses and gold chains.

On 27 May 1801 Jane wrote to Cassandra: 'The *Endymion* came into Portsmouth on Sunday, & I have sent Charles a short letter by this day's post...He has received 30£ for his share of the privateer & expects 10£ more – but of what avail is it to take prizes if he lays out the produce in presents to his Sisters. He has been buying Gold chains & Topaze Crosses for us; – he must be well scolded...I shall write again by this post to thank and reproach him. We shall be unbearably fine.'

Charles Austen, Jane's youngest brother, arrived in Portsmouth during February 1801 bearing gifts for his sisters.

111

Above left: Although the nave of the Garrison Church was badly damaged in 1941, the chancel has been restored as a memorial to the men of the garrison who lost their lives in the conflict.

Above right: The mural on the side of the present day Bridge Tavern is taken from 'Portsmouth Point' by Thomas Rowlandson, c. 1811. It satirizes the various types of lower-class boisterousness and carousing in Portsmouth harbour.

Jane uses this incident as the background for a dramatic scene in *Mansfield Park*. The crosses were purchased by Frank in Gibraltar from his share of prize money from the capture of a French vessel, the *Scipio*, in the Mediterranean off the coast of Spain. They are now on display at the Jane Austen's House Museum at Chawton.

Five miles from Portsmouth, and protecting it from the English Channel, is the Isle of Wight. In the stretch of water between, called Spithead, the ships of the Royal Navy moored to await orders. Jane used Fanny's walk along the ramparts with Henry Crawford, for a rare descriptive passage:

'The day was uncommonly lovely. It was really March; but it was April in its mild air, brisk soft wind, the bright sun, occasionally clouded for a minute; and everything looked so beautiful under the influence of such a sky, the effects of the shadows pursuing each other, on the ships at Spithead and the island beyond, with the ever-varying hues of the sea now at high water, dancing in its glee and dashing against the ramparts with so fine a sound, produced altogether such a combinations of charms for Fanny, as made her gradually almost careless of the circumstances under which she felt them. Nay, had she been without his arm, she would soon have known that she needed it.'

Alton

'I WALKED TO Alton, & dirt excepted found it delightful…' said Jane in a letter written to Cassandra on Thursday 4 February 1813.

Today Alton is promoted as Jane Austen's town and the claim is well founded. Many of the existing buildings have strong associations with her and other members of the family. For seven years, from 1809 when she moved into Chawton Cottage, Jane made frequent visits to this neat country town to consult a doctor, to shop and to visit friends and relations. During this period several members of the Austen family came to live in Alton at various times. Jane also came to the Swan Inn to collect or send parcels or to board a coach for visits further afield.

When Jane was in her teens, Alton was described as: 'a pleasant healthy town, on the Great Western Road from London through Farnham, to Southampton and the Isle of Wight. It consists of three streets, the principal of which is wide, and modern built. It has a small, but neat church; and the River Wye [Wey] runs through the town.'

Approaching Alton from Chawton, as Jane so often did, you pass a large green on the left known as The Butts. Where Butts Road becomes High Street there is a row of shops on the left comprising numbers 106 to 110. Viewed from the other side of the road, it can be seen that this was originally one building. Between 1811 and 1815 it was the home of James Hinton Baverstock after which it was rented for two years by Jane's brother Frank and his family.

In a letter dated Sunday 8 September 1816 Jane tells Cassandra: 'Our day at Alton was very pleasant, venison quite right, children well-behaved, and Mr. and Mrs. Digweed taking kindly to our charades and other games. I must also observe, for his mother's satisfaction, that Edward at my suggestion devoted himself very properly to the entertainment of Miss S. Gibson. Nothing was wanting except Mr. Sweney, but he, alas! had been ordered away to London the day before. We had a beautiful walk home by moonlight.'

When Jane was in her teens, Alton was described as 'a pleasant healthy town.'

Above: Alton High Street described in Jane's time as 'wide and modern built.'

Top right: Jane's brother Frank rented this High Street property from 1816.

Right: During February 1811 Jane accompanied Miss Beckford on a visit to see Mr Newman, apothecary and surgeon, who lived here at Lansdown House, 74 High Street.

When Baverstock sold the property in 1821 it was described as: 'An elegant VILLA RESIDENCE agreeably placed at the western extremity of the town, on the high Southampton mail road.' It had: 'a park Meadow of three acres, with Shrubbery Walk surrounding it, and a paddock of three acres adjoining.'

Mr Newman, apothecary and surgeon lived at Lansdown House, 74 High Street, on the corner of Cross & Pillory Lane, in what is now a branch of the HSBC bank. In February 1811 Jane visited him with Miss Beckford; the sister-in-law of Mr Middleton, who had a five year lease on the Great House at Chawton. Jane turned her observation of the consultation into verse:

'I've a pain in my head'
Said the suffering Beckford;
To her Doctor so dread.
'Oh! what shall I take for't?'

Said this Doctor so dread
Whose name it was Newnham.
'For this pain in your head
Ah! What can you do Ma'am?'

Said Miss Beckford, 'Suppose
If you think there's no risk,
I take a good Dose
Of calomel brisk.'—

'What a praise worthy Notion.'
Replied Mr. Newnham.
'You shall have such a potion
And so will I too Ma'am.'

In her letters Jane mentions Collyer's coach which called here at the Swan. The Alton Book Society Jane subscribed to, held their annual meetings here.

In her letters Jane mentions Collyer's coach which called at the Swan. In 1814 she wrote: 'It may never come to anything, but I must provide for the possibility, by troubling you [to] send up my Silk Pelisse by Collier on Saturday'. Just over a year later, whilst staying with her brother Henry in London she wrote: 'I want to get rid of some of my Things, & therefore shall send down a parcel by Collier on Saturday.' Collyer's coach took six and a half hours to travel to London from the Swan.

The original Swan was one third its present size when it was listed in a rental of 1499 as

Henry Austen, Jane's brother, who took Holy Orders following the collapse of his bank.

Henry Austen was a partner of the banking business of Austen, Gray and Vincent which had premises here at 10 High Street.

belonging to Thomas Cresswell. Listed in the 1674 inventory of inn holder Thomas Harrison, there were 18 chambers, a parlour, kitchen, brewhouse, malthouse, old kitchen and wine and beer cellars. The Hawkins family acquired the Swan and developed the business by having the Post Office here as well and expanding the brewery behind the main building. The Swan was also the venue for the annual meetings of the Alton Book Society to which Jane was a subscriber.

Henry Austen originally established the bank of Austen, Maunde & Austen in 1806 in Henrietta Street, London. The other Austen in the title was his brother Frank. Henry transferred part of the banking business to Hampshire. With two new partners, the bank of Austen, Gray and Vincent moved to premises at 10 High Street, Alton. The bank later moved down to 34 High Street, next to the Swan.

Dr William Curtis of Alton lived at number 4 High Street. He attended Jane in her last illness, before she went to Winchester. In April 1817, she wrote: 'my having seen Mr Curtis, or my Disorder's chusing to go away, have made me better this morning' but, by the end of May, she observed, in her last surviving letter written from Chawton, that 'Our Alton Apothy did not pretend to be able to cope with it.'

Gilbert White, the great naturalist from Selborne (5 miles south) never married, but he had seven brothers and sisters who survived to adulthood. His brother Benjamin had a daughter called Rebecca who became a friend of Jane's. Rebecca married William Parker Terry and came to live in Hill House, at Number 1 High Street, opposite the Crown Inn.

The Terry family from Dummer were old acquaintances of Jane's from Steventon. William died on 22 August 1810 and, near the first anniversary of his death, Jane dined here with Rebecca. On 31 August 1811, Jane's sister-in-law Mary (wife of brother James) noted in her diary: 'Jane and I dined at Mrs P. Terrys'. In the *Complete Poems* of James Austen we find this confirmation of his affection for Gilbert White:

'Who talks of rational delight
When Selbourne's hill appears in sight
And does not think of Gilbert White?'

Jane dined in this house at
1 High Street on 31 August 1811,
with Rebecca Terry, a niece of
Gilbert White.

Number 4 High Street, home of
Dr William Curtis, Jane's Alton
'Apothy'.

Jane Austen's friend Harry Digweed rented 'Weybourne House' at 23 Lenton Street, for a couple of years from 1809.

St Lawrence's church where children of the Lefroys, Digweeds, Terrys and Francis Austen were baptised.

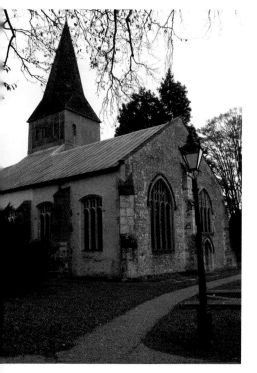

We now turn down Church Street and proceed to St Lawrence's church. Rebecca died in the summer of 1825 and is buried in a vault here along with William and their daughter Sarah who lived for only 14 weeks.

It seems likely that Jane would have been present during some of the infant baptisms which took place in St Lawrence's church. These included the children of the Lefroys, Digweeds and Terrys, all of whom were long-standing friends of the Austens. Jane's brother Francis periodically lived at Alton with his family between 1809 and 1816. His son, Francis junior, was baptized at St Lawrence's church on 8 August 1809 and, on 19 May, eight years later, the church was the venue for the baptism of his daughter Elizabeth.

Harry Digweed rented 'Weybourne House' at 23 Lenton Street, in Alton for a couple of years from 1809. The Digweeds had rented Steventon Manor when Jane was growing up at Steventon Rectory. Writing from Chawton on Wednesday 29 May 1811, Jane tells Cassandra about a get together the previous Monday evening at Weybourne House:

'…we were called upon to meet Mrs. and Miss Terry the same evening at the Digweeds; and, though Anna was of course invited too, I think it always safest to keep her away from the family lest she should be doing too little or too much. Mrs. Terry, Mary, and Robert, with my aunt Harding and her daughter, came from Dummer for a day and a night - all very agreeable and very much delighted with the new house and with Chawton in general.'

On 9 July 1816 Jane wrote a lively letter to her nephew Edward while he was at Winchester School. In it she mentions a change of servants at Chawton Cottage: 'Do you know that our Browning is gone? You must prepare for a William when you come, a good-looking lad, civil and quiet, and seeming likely to do.'

The William here is William Littleworth who was born at 'The Nutshell', 33 Lenten Street and baptized at St Lawrence's church in 1795. This means he must have been about twenty-one when Jane is writing about him. The 1851 census shows William and his wife Mary still living at Chawton Cottage, six years after Cassandra's death.

John White of Chawton, who died in 1921 at the age of 100, is recorded as saying: 'I remember a nice dog, his name was 'Link', that she [Cassandra] had. He always went with her manservant, William Littleworth, to Chawton House for milk, and carried it home in his mouth.'

Between 1808 and 1810, when Francis Austen was abroad with the Navy, he settled his family in a house at 31 Lenten Street, now known as 'The Old House'. During April 1809,

'The Nutshell', 33 Lenten Street birthplace of William Littleworth, who was for many years the Austen's manservant at Chawton Cottage.

Between 1808 and 1810, when Francis Austen was abroad with the Navy, he settled his family in The Old House at 31 Lenten Street.

Wyards Farm was home to Jane's niece and her husband, Anna and Benjamin Lefroy, with whom Jane often exchanged visits.

Jane's mother fell ill whilst staying at an inn in Alton (probably The George). Fanny Knight, Jane's niece, recorded that during Mrs Austen's recovery she was: 'able to move from the Inn to a cottage of Mrs. F. Austens close to the town (where she is settled for the two years her husband expects to be absent. He is gone to China, & she is to be confined in June).'

On 7 July 1809 Mrs Austen, Cassandra and Jane moved into Chawton Cottage. Five days later, Francis's son, Francis junior, was born in The Old House in Lenten Street. The first surviving letter of Jane's written at Chawton includes a poem to her brother which begins:
'My dearest Frank, I wish you Joy
Of Mary's safety with a boy.'

The next property of interest is a little way out of the town. Continue down Lenten Street until it becomes Basingstoke Road. At the junction with the A339 turn right and then first left along the lane that leads to Wyards Farm. Stephen Terry from Dummer leased this lovely seventeenth-century house from 1811 to 1814.

Anna Lefroy, James's daughter by his first marriage was an aspiring novelist and a particular favourite niece of Jane's. Following her marriage in November 1814 to Benjamin Lefroy, the couple rented a few rooms in Wyards Farmhouse, the main part being occupied by the farm bailiff and his family.

Biographers have speculated that there was much of Anna in Jane's portrayal of Emma Woodhouse; clever and attractive but possessing 'the power of having rather too much of her own way.' Wyards was an easy walk from Chawton Cottage and Jane became a frequent visitor. She mentions the house in a letter of Friday 29 September 1815:

'We told Mr. B. Lefroy, that if the weather did not prevent us we should certainly come and see you to-morrow and bring Cassy, [a child of Charles Austen whose wife had recently died] trusting to your being good enough to give her a dinner about one o'clock, that we might be able to be with you the earlier and stay the longer; but on giving Cassy her choice of the Fair or Wyards she has preferred the former, which we trust will not greatly affront you - if it does you may hope that some little Anna, hereafter, may revenge the insult by a similar preference of an Alton fair to her cousin Cassy.'

There is a unique opportunity for Jane Austen fans to stay at Wyards; a house described by Nigel Nicholson as 'delectable'. Mrs Ann Monk, the present owner, offers a quintessential English B&B.

Anna Lefroy, James Austen's daughter, painted in 1845 when she was fifty-two.

Chawton Cottage & Village

EDWARD, THE third of the eight Austen children was born on 7 October 1768 at Deane. When he was twelve years old he was formally presented to Thomas and Catherine Knight, who were wealthy relatives of his father. Thomas had given George Austen the living at Steventon in 1761.

Despite having considerable wealth and a happy marriage, the Knights were childless. It was a common practice in those days for distant branches of families to foster a child to give them a better start in life, even though both parents were still alive. As with Fanny Price in *Mansfield Park*, it was an arrangement that was agreeable to all parties. Edward was to spend his time studying under his father's tuition at Steventon and spend his holidays with his newly acquired family in Kent.

The Knights eventually adopted Edward in 1783, he became their legal heir and subsequently changed his surname to Knight. By 1807 Edward had inherited the Knight estates and had a family of eleven children of his own. In 1808, two weeks after giving birth to their last baby, Edward's wife Elizabeth died suddenly.

Topaz crosses Charles bought for Jane and Cassandra with his prize money from the capture of the French ship *La Tribune* are on display here at Chawton House Museum.

In his bereavement Edward sought to be closer to his mother and sisters who were at the time living in Southampton, in the rented house in Castle Square, with Frank and his wife. Edward offered a house on either the Godmersham estate, close to his home in Kent, or on the Hampshire estate at Chawton. Mrs Austen was in favour of Kent, but was persuaded by Jane, Cassandra and Martha Lloyd to choose Hampshire.

With the exception of Steventon where she grew up, Chawton, in north-east Hampshire, was where Jane found the most security and peace in her life. The village was on a main coaching route from London which passed through Alton and divided just outside their new home. The right fork went to Winchester and Southampton and the left fork to Fareham and Gosport. Today the main road bypasses Chawton and the village and it has a quiet, rather timeless air.

The Cottage (as it became to be known to the family) had actually been built in the seventeenth century as an inn, to take advantage of its strategic roadside position. It is an irregular two storey, red brick building with six bedrooms and extra garrets in the tiled roof-space for servant's quarters.

There are other domestic outbuildings set around a small courtyard and a garden for vegetables, fruit and flowers. Cassandra and Mary Lloyd shared the main housekeeping duties, leaving Mrs Austen to busy herself with gardening during the day and knitting and patchwork in the evening. Edward also provided the ladies with a donkey-cart so they could drive into Alton for visiting and shopping.

Opposite: Jane's Chawton Cottage where she lived from July 1809 until May 1817 is now Chawton House Museum and is administered by the Jane Austen Memorial Trust.

Across the road from Chawton Cottage is a small timber framed house with red brick infill, appropriately named Thatched Cottage. During the Austens' time in the village the cottage was home to Miss Benn, a poor spinster living in reduced circumstances.

Space in the courtyard outbuildings with the bakehouse and wash boiler is shared by the donkey-cart Jane used for shopping trips to Alton.

Opposite: Thatched Cottage, home to poor Miss Benn.

All Saints' church at nearby Farringdon where Reverend John Benn held the living.

Although she is mentioned in Jane Austen's letters more than a dozen times we know little about her. Some biographers have speculated that because of her poverty she was frequently invited to the Chawton Cottage for meals and may have been a model for Miss Bates in *Emma*.

Miss Benn was the sister of Reverend John Benn who held the living of All Saints' church at nearby Farringdon from 1797 to 1857. John Benn and his wife had a dozen children, which probably meant they could not do much to help Miss Benn. 'Harriet Benn,' wrote Jane Austen, 'sleeps at the Great House to-night and spends to-morrow with us; and the plan is that we should all walk with her to drink tea at Farringdon.'

At Chawton Jane was at last in a peaceful and congenial environment to return to her writing. Her daily routine included rising early and practising simple songs and country dances on her pianoforte. Then she prepared a nine o'clock breakfast for the family. Her days were then filled with sewing, embroidery, walking, shopping and with entertaining

Above: Treasures, artifacts and displays help give an idea of life in the cottage in the early 1800s.

Top right: The drawing room at Chawton Cottage as it is today.

The newly refurbished kitchen has been beautifully renovated and is sometimes used for cooking events.

the ever-growing number of nephews and nieces who called or stayed at the cottage.

Whenever she could Jane made time for writing; not in a room of her own but in the communal living room with a door opening directly onto the street. Her modest little writing table, where she penned some of the greatest novels in the English language, is still there. It is said that the other door from the room, leading to the back of the house, creaked and she asked that it should not be oiled. The noise alerted her that someone was approaching so she could quickly slip her small sheets of paper out of sight and so keep her authorship a secret.

Around the autumn of 1810, Jane was ready to submit *Sense & Sensibility* to Thomas Egerton of Whitehall and it was accepted for publication at the author's expense. At the end of March 1811 she was able to correct some proof sheets while staying with Henry and Eliza in London. The novel appeared in the following October. The title page merely showed it as being 'By a Lady'.

Meanwhile, down in Portsmouth, the wife of a navy clerk who worked in the dockyard pay office, was giving birth to their second child. The boy, born on 7 February 1812, was to make his own impact on the literary world. His name was Charles John Huffam Dickens.

Jane's modest little writing table where she penned some of the greatest novels in the English language.

The first edition of *Sense & Sensibility* was sold out by July 1813. Next Jane turned her attention to revising *First Impressions* written fifteen years earlier. She 'lop't and crop't' the text, and changed the title to *Pride & Prejudice*. This time Egerton showed no hesitation and bought the copyright from her for £110. The book appeared at the end of January 1813 and there was a demand for a second edition by the autumn. The title page read 'By the Author of *Sense & Sensibility*'.

By the New Year of 1813 Jane was already halfway through *Mansfield Park*, the first of her mature novels to be written and published straight off, without any revisions or delays. Having never been to Northamptonshire, she had to write around to enquire if it was a country of hedgerows. But her knowledge of Portsmouth gained while living in nearby

Southampton provided her with the detail for Fanny Price's miserable experience when visiting her parental home.

Jane probably finished the text of *Mansfield Park* in the autumn of 1813 and the book was published by Egerton, in May 1814. Even before it was published she started on *Emma*. Jane's authorship was now an open secret in London largely due to Henry's proud acknowledgements of his sister's name. This led to the Prince of Wales, who was a great fan, asking if her next novel could be dedicated to him. A request like this could not be refused despite the fact that Jane thoroughly disapproved of the Prince Regent's extravagant and immoral life style.

Jane's creative flow was in full flood. Using memories of her recent life in Bath and holidays in Lyme Regis, she now began to write *Persuasion*. The narrative is set against a post-war background when Royal Navy officers, like her own brothers, were being paid off and looking for a more settled life in the country. Early in 1816 Jane's health began to deteriorate and a year later she was forced to leave her beloved Chawton Cottage to seek expert medical help in Winchester.

She was never to return to the house of which eight years earlier she had joyously described as:

'Our Chawton home, how much we find
Already in it, to our mind;
And how convinced that when complete
It will all other houses beat
That ever have been made or mended,
With rooms concise, or rooms distended.'

Cassandra was destined to long outlive her sister Jane. She continued on at Chawton with regular visits to her brothers, nieces and nephews. In 1827 Mrs Austen died and was buried in the Chawton cemetery. Soon thereafter (in about 1828) Martha Lloyd also left the household, this time to marry Cassandra's younger brother Frank, then Admiral Sir Francis Austen. Cassandra continued living alone in the cottage until her death at the age of seventy-two.

Cassandra, Jane's beloved sister.

Chawton House Library & Church

IN CHAWTON VILLAGE there are two primary properties associated with the Austens known by the family as the Cottage (where Jane lived) and the Great House, which is a five minute walk away down the old road. Today the Cottage is officially known as the 'Jane Austen House Museum' and the Great House as 'Chawton House Library'.

Chawton House Library is set in 275 acres of Hampshire countryside, and is used today for conferences, filming and more recently as a venue for weddings.

Left: The family silhouette depicting the moment when the twelve-year-old Edward was officially presented to Thomas and Catherine Knight.

Below: The full-length portrait of Edward Austen painted during the time of his Grand Tour of Europe.

This lovely contemporary painting of Chawton Great House, farm and church, hangs on the upper landing.

The Library is now 'The Centre for the Study of Early English Women's Writing: 1600-1830'. It was established by American entrepreneur and philanthropist Sandy Lerner and opened to the public in 2003. The library has a collection of over 9,000 books, together with related original manuscripts. It also houses the Knight Collection of books belonging to the family who owned the Great House for 400 years. This part of the collection was inherited by Jane's brother Edward and Jane is known to have enjoyed access to these precious volumes.

On a wall in the dining room of the Great House is a family silhouette depicting the moment that changed Edward's fortunes. Edward, the third of the eight Austen children, was born on 7 October 1768 at Deane. When he was twelve years old he was officially presented to Thomas and Catherine Knight, who were wealthy relatives of his father. Adjacent to the silhouette is a full-length portrait of Edward when he was in his early twenties. It was painted in Rome during the time of his Grand Tour of Europe.

Thomas had given Revd George Austen the living at Steventon in 1761. The Knights subsequently adopted Edward. When he eventually inherited the estates, he changed his surname to Knight. This was an accepted practice at the time, in the same way that Lovelace Wither became Lovelace Bigg-Wither when he inherited the Manydown estate.

The Great Hall is the Library's main reception room used today for conferences, lectures, seminars and Regency dancing.

Edward lived on the Knight's Kentish estate at Godmersham where he brought up his family. During most of his ownership of the Chawton estate he leased the Great House to tenants and made six monthly management calls. During his trip to Hampshire in April 1807 the tenant at the time, a Mr Coulthard, had just vacated the property. This gave Edward the opportunity to bring the older members of his family to Chawton for a holiday. They came for a fortnight at the end of August, partly to install young Edward for his first term at Winchester College.

Jane came from Southampton with her mother and sister, and James brought his family as well. On this occasion the house party stayed ten days, exploring the rambling house and its estate. When calling on neighbours and tenants in the village and shopping in Alton Jane obviously saw the Cottage but had no reason at that time to think it would ever be her home.

James's daughter Fanny has left us with a description of the Great House at the time of the 1807 family get together:

'This is a fine old house, built long before Queen Elizabeth, I believe & here are such a number of old irregular passages & &c that it is very entertaining to explore them, & often when I think myself miles away from one part of the house I find a passage or entrance close to it, & don't know when I shall be quite mistress of all the intricate, & different ways.'

The Great House was let again to tenants for a period of five years shortly before the Austen ladies moved in to the Cottage. It was free once more in 1813 and Edward brought his entire family to live there for five months while Godmersham was being repainted.

The Great Hall is the Library's main reception room, used today for conferences, lectures, seminars and Regency dancing. It dates from the first phase of construction, started by John Knight in 1583. The fireback in the recently discovered fireplace at the north end of the room is inscribed 'JK 1588' and commemorates John Knight's contribution of £50 towards the cost of fighting the Spanish Armada.

We know that Jane dined here at the table we see today. A fragment of a letter remains which she wrote on 2 March 1815 to her niece Caroline who was nine at the time:

'... we four sweet Brothers & Sisters dine today at the Great House. Is not that quite natural? — Grandmama & Miss Lloyd will be by themselves, I do not exactly know what they will have for dinner, very likely somepork? - Do you know that ... '

Opposite: We know that Jane dined here at the table we see today.

The Great Gallery was originally used for exercise by the ladies of the house.

The 'Ladies Withdrawing Room' where Jane liked to sit to keep an eye on who was passing and visiting.

The 'Ladies Withdrawing Room' or 'panelled embrasure' in the corner of the Oak Room is located over the porch. It offers an excellent view down the drive and Jane liked to sit here keeping an eye on who was passing along the old road and who was visiting the house.

At the far end of the drive, on the other side of the old road, is Chawton Rectory. The Reverend John Papillon was rector here when the Austen ladies moved to the village. Mrs Knight, Edward's adopted mother, suggested that John Papillon would be a good catch for Jane. On Friday 9 December 1808 Jane wrote to Cassandra: 'I am very much obliged to Mrs. Knight for such a proof of the interest she takes in me, and she may depend upon it that I will marry Mr. Papillon, whatever may be his reluctance or my own. I owe her much more than such a trifling sacrifice.'

An Austen family in-joke was that the Reverend John Papillon who lived here at Chawton Rectory would be a good catch for Jane.

Jane regularly attended St Nicholas's church, however a disastrous fire in 1871 effectively destroyed most of the building she would have known.

Mrs Austen and Cassandra are buried next to each other in the churchyard near the south wall of the church.

Jane regularly attended St Nicholas's church which is situated to the right of the drive, as you approach the Great House. A church has stood on this site since at least 1270, however a disastrous fire in 1871 effectively destroyed the building except for the chancel. Jane mentions the church but the only part she would recognise today is the chancel. The present nave, north aisle, vestry and tower date from 1872/3 although many of the early memorials were saved and are still on the walls.

The graves of Mrs Austen and Cassandra are next to each other in the churchyard near the south wall of the church. In the nave there is a memorial to Jane's mother, who died at Chawton in 1827 aged eighty-seven. It was erected by her children Edward, Henry, Francis, Charles and Cassandra.

Winchester

IN 1809, WHEN Jane came to live at Chawton, her new home was 17 miles from Winchester. Without suitable transport or support from male members of the family, a daytrip was never a viable option. Opportunities of sightseeing, shopping and attending evening balls in the big city could not be considered. However, the situation was somewhat compensated for by the fact that the bustling little town of Alton was within walking distance.

Jane did have links with Winchester from her early life as certain of her nephews attended Winchester College. The cathedral's assistant organist, George Chard, used regularly to ride to the Steventon neighbourhood to provide piano lessons for Jane and others. Austen family members bought books from John Burdon's shop at 11 College Road. The shop, which supplied books to the college, is still there. Now called P & G Wells, it stands a couple of doors away from the house in which Jane spent her last days.

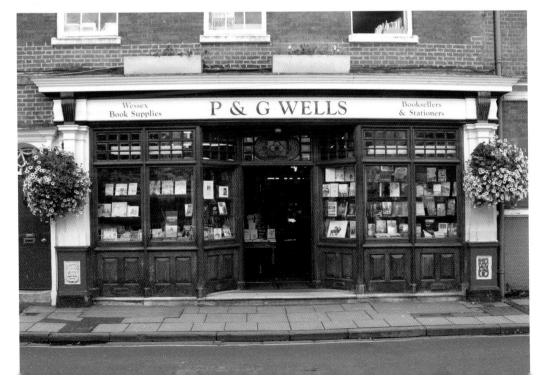

Number 11 College Street, next door but two from the house where Jane spent the last days of her life, is P & G Wells bookshop. In Jane's time the proprietor was John Burden from whom the Austen family members purchased books.

The Prebendary House at Number 10 in the Close is the cathedral's current education centre. Jane's friend Elizabeth Bigg lived here during the first two years of her marriage to the Reverend William Heathcote.

We have already met Elizabeth Bigg, a friend of Jane's from the Steventon days who was one of the younger daughters of Mr Lovelace Bigg-Wither of Manydown Park near Basingstoke. In 1798 Elizabeth married the Reverend William Heathcote, a canon of the cathedral. The couple took up residence in the Prebendary House at Number 10 the Close which now serves as the education centre.

After a couple of years the Heathcotes moved to number 2 (now demolished) where they stayed a further two years until William's death in 1802. By this time Elizabeth had a young son and she moved back with him to live with her family at Manydown. There is a possibility Jane may have visited Winchester at some time during the four years between 1798 and 1802 when Elizabeth was living in the city but there is no record of it.

Just over a decade later, Elizabeth had a second period of residence in the city and this time Jane is known to have visited. Lovelace Bigg-Wither died in 1813 and his son Harris inherited Manydown. Elizabeth moved back to Winchester where by this time her son was attending the college. The Dean and Chapter made Number 12 Cathedral Close (now re-numbered 11) available to her and she moved in together with her sister Alethea.

The following year Jane, accompanied by Cassandra and Martha Lloyd, came to visit their old friends. They stayed for a week in the imposing red brick house in the Close, from Boxing Day 1814 until 2 January 1815.

Cheyney Court, adjoining the Priory Gate on the Close side, is also fifteenth century and was once the Bishops' Court House. Jane would have been familiar with this beautiful building from her visit of 1814 and also her brief excursion in a sedan chair.

This elegant red brick house, set back in the north-west corner of the Close, dates from the 1660s and is now privately rented from the Dean and Chapter. Jane and Cassandra stayed here for a week's visit at the end of 1814.

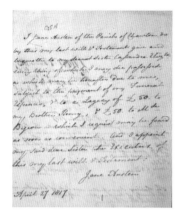

Jane Austen's last will and testament.

Early in 1816, when Jane was forty, friends and family members started to notice a change in her manner. She became more serious and reflective. As the year progressed she began to suffer from fever and weakness. In May, accompanied by Cassandra, she visited Cheltenham but did not find the waters beneficial. In July she finished the first version of *Persuasion* and subsequently made brilliant revisions to the last three chapters.

In January 1817 Jane reported she was well enough to walk to Alton without fatigue but by March she was sitting down and resting for periods during her walks. By April she was an armchair-bound invalid. After some weeks of confinement with nausea and back pains she felt she needed to make her will. She left everything to Cassandra apart from fifty pounds to Henry and another fifty to his housekeeper who had lost her savings when he was bankrupted. The will reads:

'I Jane Austen of the Parish of Chawton do by this my last Will & Testament give and bequeath to my dearest Sister Cassandra Elizth every thing of which I may die possessed, or which may be hereafter due to me, subject to the payment of my Funeral Expences, & to a Legacy of £ 50. to my Brother Henry, & £ 50. to Mde Bigeon–which I request may be paid as soon as convenient. And I appoint my said dear Sister the Executrix of this my last Will & Testament.'

Jane had been under the care of William Curtis, the apothecary at Alton. He eventually concluded he could do no more for her and recommended she seek help from Mr Giles King Lyford, the eminent head surgeon at the new hospital in Parchment Road, Winchester.

It was Elizabeth who arranged lodgings for Jane and Cassandra at 8 College Road, one of the rental properties owned by a Mrs David. Looking at Elizabeth's huge house, located inside the Close, one wonders why she didn't have her invalid friend to stay with her there. At the time she was on her own because Alethea was visiting Switzerland. Perhaps there was still some resentment from the time when Jane accepted a proposal of marriage from Elizabeth's young brother Harris and changed her mind the following day. In any event, Elizabeth did visit Jane every day at 8 College Street.

On a wet Saturday in May, Jane and Cassandra made the journey from Chawton to Winchester. They travelled in James's coach, with Henry and her young nephew William Knight escorting them on horseback. The positive move made her feel better and she reported that her lodgings were very comfortable and the view from the bay-window in the neat little drawing room overlooked Dr Gabell's garden.

The house at 8 College Street where Jane Austen spent the last eight weeks of her life. England's greatest female novelist was just forty-one when she died here in the arms of her beloved sister Cassandra.

Jane had periods of remission and on one occasion felt well enough to venture out in a sedan chair. Her condition, now generally thought to be Addison's disease, was incurable at the time and Lyford was ultimately unable to do anything for her. In the early hours of Friday 18 July Jane died peacefully with her head on Cassandra's shoulder. She was just forty-one. The bond between the sisters caused Cassandra to write:

'I have lost a treasure, such a sister, such a friend as never can have been surpassed. She was the sun of my life, the gilder of every pleasure, the soother of every sorrow; I had not a thought concealed from her, and it is as if I had lost a part of myself. I loved her only too well — not better than she deserved, but I am conscious that my affection for her made me sometimes unjust to and negligent of others…'

On the following Thursday Jane's coffin was conveyed to the cathedral,

On Thursday 24 July 1817, Cassandra watched from the little bay-window as Jane's funeral procession moved along College Street to turn the corner and pass through Kingsgate.

The fifteenth-century Priory Gate is the main entrance to the Close. Jane's cortège passed through here on its way to the cathedral.

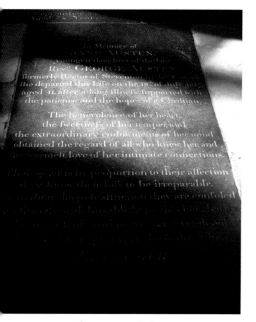

Afternoon sunlight streams in through the west window illuminating Jane's grave. She lies under the floor of the north aisle of the nave, where you can still see her simple gravestone. The inscription records her personal virtues and stoicism, but makes no mention of her writing.

accompanied by her brothers, Edward, Henry and Frank and her nephew James Edward. At the time women did not often attend funerals so Cassandra remained in the house. From the bay-window she had a view of the little procession along the length of College Street until they turned under the arch of Kingsgate.

Today, tourists come from all over the world to stand by Jane Austen's grave. Nearby they can also see her brass plaque and memorial window – three testaments to a remarkable woman whose novels so brilliantly capture the quiet drama of human relationships.

Looking round this vast impressive space the question remains; how did Jane come to be buried in the cathedral? She was not a native of the city, nor at that time was she a person of sufficient eminence to warrant such an honour. Could it be that brother Henry let the Dean and Chapter know of his sister's connection to the Prince of Wales, of his admiration of Jane's works (he had a copy of her novels in each of his homes) and of the dedication of *Emma* to the Prince?

There has been a cathedral in Winchester since about 648 AD. The foundations of the present cathedral were laid out in 1079 by Walkelin, the first Norman Bishop. To this new building (consecrated in 1093) the relics of St Swithin were solemnly transferred. Winchester is one of the largest cathedrals in England, with the longest nave and greatest overall length of any Gothic cathedral in Europe.

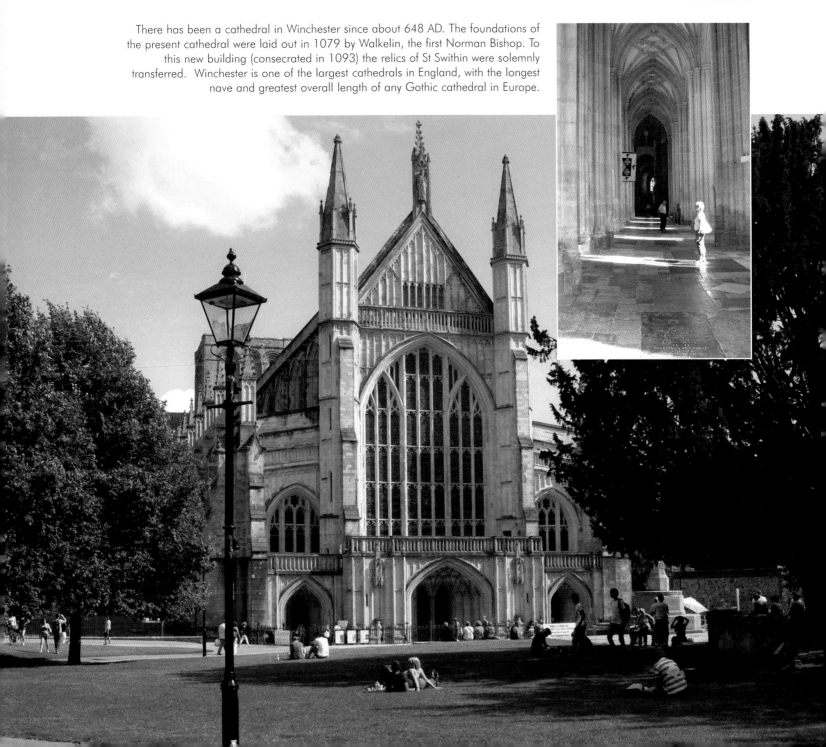

Selected Bibliography

A Chronology of Jane Austen and Her Family 1600-2000	Deirdre Le Faye
Alton's Inns	Jane Hurst
A Memoir of Jane Austen	J.E. Austen-Leigh
Ashe & Deane	Richard Tanner
Inns of Andover	H.W. Earney
In the steps of Jane Austen	Anne-Marie Edwards
Jane Austen – A Family Record	Deirdre Le Faye
Jane Austen – A Life	Claire Tomalin
Jane Austen and Alton	Jane Hurst
Overton in Regency Times	Richard Waldram
The World of Jane Austen	Nigel Nicolson